INVESTMENT SURVIVAL

How to Use Investment Research to Create Winning Portfolios for the Coming Bull Market

Rod Hagenbuch
&
Richard J. Capalbo

with Jilleen R. Westbrook, Ph.D.

This publication is designed to provide accurate and authoritative
information in regard to the subject matter covered. It is sold with
the understanding that the publisher is not engaged in rendering
legal, accounting, or other professional services. If legal advice or
other expert assistance is required, the services of a competent
professional person should be sought

ISBN 0-9725769-0-8
Printed by Sinclair Printing Company, Los Angeles

First Edition

We dedicate this book to one of
Wall Street's giants,
I.W. Burnham,
who truly understood the value of good
investment research and certainly knew
how to use it.
We will miss his wisdom.

Rod Hagenbuch
and
Richard J. Capalbo

CONTENTS

Investment Survival

Table of Contents

ABOUT THE AUTHORS

Rod Hagenbuch is co-founder of The Quantum Leap Institute and Quantum Leap Securities. He is a graduate of Michigan State University, and has lectured at the Securities Industry Institute (SII) at the Wharton School at the University of Pennsylvania. Rod's professional experience includes 32 years in the securities industry with Merrill Lynch as an institutional consultant and branch manager. He has worked extensively with securities research analysts, consults with buy-side institutions, and has trained securities brokers on using securities research for over 20 years. Rod lives with his wife, LaVerne, and dogs in Pacific Palisades, California.

Richard Capalbo is a co-founder of The Quantum Leap Institute and Quantum Leap Securities. He attended undergraduate at Fordham University, and received his MA from Wharton Business School. Richard served as the director of marketing for Drexel Burnham Lambert, the CEO and President of Bateman Eichler and was Chairman of the Securities Industry Institute at Wharton. He has consulted with many asset management firms and has served as the marketing director for Merrill Lynch in Southern California. Richard has lectured extensively in the securities industry and at the SII at Wharton. He lives with his wife, Kathleen, and family in Pasadena, California.

Jilleen Westbrook, Ph.D. received her undergraduate degree in economics from University of California, Davis, and her M.A. and Ph.D. in economics from the Claremont Graduate University. She has taught economics and finance at Temple University, University of Southern California and The Claremont Colleges. She is a consultant and writer and lives with her husband, Rick Roberts, and two children in San Marino, California.

INTRODUCTION

The year 2002 has not been good for the financial community. As we write, the United States is experiencing major scandals involving securities analysts, major accounting firms and corporate managers, plus conflicts of interest in the investment banking industry. The press is targeting the Securities Exchange Commission (SEC) as being ineffective. Even Martha Stewart, a person who represents all that is wholesome in America, is being accused of insider trading.

Between 1999 and 2002, we witnessed paper fortunes disappear as certain sectors of the stock market tumbled. Some investors lost 80 percent on their investments because their stock portfolios were significantly divergent from their intended benchmarks.

If an investor fails to learn how to pick stocks that

contribute to his portfolio coming to resemble a carefully considered benchmark, it is highly unlikely that he will ever reach his investment objectives. One cannot survive in the stock market without adequate knowledge of stock sectors and stock portfolio construction. The name of the game is "Investment Survival," and this book provides impartial information about how to survive turbulent markets and the bull markets that will eventually come again.

Investing in the stock market during uncertain times can turn even the bravest among us timid. During the early 21st century, the perils involved with the stock market have led many investors to consider moving their investments from stocks to cash and bonds. Even though statistical evidence shows that stocks out-perform bonds and cash over the longer-term, stock market volatility can encourage investors to hold "safer" assets. For most investors, from a person with many years until retirement to a retiree, the "safer" approach is probably not the best approach when considering the risk/return trade-off. In order to succeed at investing, investors need to develop strategies for success. As life spans increase, investors often need to own more aggressive securities in order to ensure a comfortable retirement.

While stocks are good long-term investments, creating an excellent portfolio of stocks is not easy. There is a huge amount of information available to the investor about publicly-traded companies. In fact, there is so much information that many investors make poor decisions about their portfolios by misusing the information, or by not using any investment information because they are totally overwhelmed by the sheer volume of it all.

Introduction

The information age offers a wealth of Web sites, books, magazines and other publications providing stock information and recommendations, but a random approach to purchasing stocks based on that information often leads to an unbalanced, very risky stock portfolio with lackluster performance. Investors want good places to invest their hard-earned money. Investors are constantly searching for the next great idea or "real thing." The problem for the investor is to identify the real thing when he comes across it.

The plethora of research information can be overwhelming and misleading. The volume and inconsistent formats across research sources greatly diminish the usefulness of the existing research. We believe that it takes several different types of research and points of view, organized in a precise manner, to find investment success. By having more than one information source, it is akin to getting a second and third opinion before undertaking a serious medical procedure. We have developed a process that is straight forward and provides results.

The ultimate goal of this book is to educate the reader, whether he is a stockbroker, investment advisor or investor, about the use of quality investment information and its use in portfolio construction. There has never been a more important time to become educated about investment information. A well-constructed portfolio will lead to investing success. We identify the elements of investment research that have real value and show how to identify and organize the information so that brokers and investors can build solid performing equity portfolios. Surviving in the investment world involves knowing where to look for good research, learning the disciplines of how to assemble a balanced portfolio, monitoring the portfolio and applying the disciplines over time. It also means avoiding the useless information that is so readily available in the media.

Why our Approach is Needed Now: a Little Background

The securities industry has gone through massive changes in the past 30 years. Brokers, investors and securities analysts have all been greatly affected by these changes. The economics of the bear market in the early 1970s forced out almost half of all registered representatives working for brokerage houses. Many of those that left the industry took with them a great deal of experience and knowledge about the market and managing investments. In 1975 negotiated commissions were introduced, laying the foundation for deep discounts for institutions and the beginning of discount, and subsequently, on-line brokerage firms. A very volatile market in the 1970s led to a 45 percent market decline. The subsequent recovery left the market at about the same level as it was at the start of the decade. In addition, we witnessed the highest nominal interest rates in the history of the United States. When interest rates started to drop in the early 1980s, the economy began to recover and the securities market experienced the biggest upside run in the century. Bondholders earned the highest total returns in memory as interest rates dropped and the value of bonds increased sharply.

With clients again earning positive returns, brokerage firms began to rapidly grow their sales forces. As stock prices rose sharply in the 1980s, except for a brief period in 1987, most investors made money. During the same period, the number of mutual funds expanded rapidly. The latter part of the 1980s and early 1990s witnessed the explosive growth of individual professionally-managed accounts offered to clients in a single "wrap" pricing structure. Packaged products became much more prevalent. Clients and brokers were happy, but when the post-1999 stock market correction occurred, many faced dramatic losses. In many cases, those losses were greater than they had to be, because clients lacked knowledge about the risks associated with their portfolios.

Many investors held portfolios that were overly concentrated in narrow parts of the market. Financial advisors often were unable to help clients effectively because the clients' holdings were now less transparent, since so much wealth was held in the form of packaged products or in the hands of professional managers. To make matters worse, clients often purchased securities on their own without the help of their advisors, taking advice from Web sites and "hot stock" tips. Only the most experienced financial advisors were able to control all of their client's assets and ensure that those assets were kept in proper balance. We would like to see every professional financial advisor acquire the skills necessary to manage client's assets effectively in the face of such rapid changes and easy access to stock market information.

Beyond managing a client's portfolio needs, the information age and changes in the marketplace necessitate that brokers work more efficiently. Doing so has never been more difficult. While consulting with brokers from many different securities firms, we found that almost every financial advisor was confronted with an overload of information. Advisors benefit from a systematic approach to managing information. Such an approach allows advisors more time with their clients and time to emphasize on the research that is important for risk management and excellent stock selection.

Why we are Uniquely Qualified

We each have 30-plus years of hands-on investment and management experience. In this book, we talk about investors both working alone and with financial advisors as partners. We are convinced that two heads are better than one. We started working as a team while managing a very large, complex branch office for Merrill Lynch in Los Angeles, California. We have subsequently had success working together in several types of businesses. When a real, trusting, working relationship is developed, better answers and better results are achieved. Beyond our relationship with each other, we each have an excellent relationship with our financial advisors. Because of — and in spite of — our extensive investment experience, we would not think about investing without the advice of an outstanding financial advisor.

The investor/advisor relationship goes far beyond caring for the financial portfolio. We help each other with medical referrals, charity funding, legal sources and business referrals. Our advisor knows everything about our finances, individually and for our company. Our wives know that should anything happen to us they should call our financial advisor. We know that he would take care of anything our families needed. We believe an investor/advisor relationship is one of the most important a person can develop, when there is trust and mutual concern beyond simply making money in the markets.

Introduction

When we formed our consulting company The Quantum Leap Institute in 1999, we began to work with both mutual fund companies and the largest advisors in brokerage firms. In our consulting practice, we found many of the advisors servicing clients had little or no formal training in investing. We found that some of the most important skills in investment management were not well understood. After surveying the currently available books and the most frequently used Internet sources, we found a great deal of information, both general and specific, but little was practical enough to help anyone actually manage investments. Our clients told us that there was a crying need for investment education for both financial advisors and investors. The information in this book has been assembled from many sources, but is primarily a result of our own experience and knowledge servicing institutions and training advisors.

We have been fortunate to have had outstanding associates, role models and mentors in our careers. We were both privileged to work with some of the top minds on Wall Street, in professional investment management and in academia. We also learned a great deal by listening to the feedback from hundreds of outstanding practicing financial advisors over a 15-year period, suggesting improvements to the process we were presenting and describe in this book. We were heavily involved with performance measurement and the application of modern portfolio theory (MPT) in the investment community during the early 1970s, when these issues were new and then became the cutting edge in investment practices. We have maintained an active interest in the evolution of portfolio theory and its applications since then.

The Organization of the Book

In Chapter 1, we discuss the evolution of the broker-age business, the growth of discount brokerages, Internet trading and the changing role of the stockbroker. It has become obvious to us that many investors are doing their own thing with investing, and many are not doing it very well. Several million individuals are now trading on-line without the help of professionals. The problem with this approach is that investors are often disconnected from knowledge-based, disciplined investment practices, mis-understanding many of the investment "bets" they are making. They often focus on what was hot last year.

Risk analysis has now become so mainstream that few professionals would even think of leaving risk out of any analysis of performance. Risk-adjusted return is now a standard in the industry. Many advisors and investors have a fair understanding of the concept of risk as measured by beta and standard deviation, but they sometimes forget to manage risk through diversification in constructing portfolios. They can have a mix of value and growth stocks in the portfolio, they can have both "large cap" and "small cap" stocks, but still end up ***dramatically*** out of balance with market sectors, which is the greatest portfolio risk. Along these lines, the topics of asset allocation, risk and diversification are discussed in Chapter 2, and the topic of portfolio styles is discussed at length in Chapter 4.

Historically, a great deal of training for new bro-kers was focused on how to invest in individual stocks. Individual stock trading was the bread and butter of a broker's and brokerage firm's business. Mutual funds were a thing of the future, and major brokerage firms didn't allow their brokers to sell mutual fund products. The focus on individual stocks can lead to investment practices devoid of structure. We discuss why the focus upon individual stocks is not the optimal approach in Chapter 3. Individual companies are the building blocks of portfolios. They are parts of a whole. In highly-unusual cases, people get wealthy by focusing solely on individual stocks without care for the portfolio. These lucky people bear tremendous risk, and at times are compensated for doing so. They also run the risk of extreme losses. Individual stocks are a vehicle for proper equity allocation in structured portfolios.

Chapters 5 through 8 together discuss these investment disciplines using sources of unique securities research, and provide applications. As an example, Chapter 9 develops part of a portfolio from scratch using the discipline developed in the earlier chapters. Chapter 10 explains how to use the process to manage a portfolio over time, and Chapter 11 discusses some advanced topics such as global investing and hedge funds.

Final Thoughts and Acknowledgments

Financial advisors must educate themselves and their clients about risk management and the portfolio approach. We do not think that financial advisors can properly advise clients about managed investments if they do not have the tools to understand portfolio construction and proper diversification themselves. There are tremendous pressures on managers of both mutual funds and professional accounts to chase investing styles that are currently out-performing and in market favor. We have seen professional managers with excellent long-term records sell their firms and then watch the new portfolio manager place 50 percent of an entire portfolio into technology stocks at the worst possible time. Financial advisors must understand what is happening to the professionally-managed portfolios that they have recommended to their clients. To do this, they must understand professional portfolio management themselves.

We argue in this book for a long-term approach to investing. Today, everyone is bombarded by 24-hour television programs featuring top analyst and portfolio managers, quoting the latest numbers on sales, earnings, consumer confidence, inflation, deficits and Federal Reserve actions. Web sites have daily and hourly updates on new information and recommendations. All of this information is useless because the time frame is far too short, and because it is out of context. One bit of information has no relation to the next and none of it is related to a long-term comprehensive portfolio. Portfolios require management to be successful in the long-term. The average length of service of the CEOs in the Fortune 1000 companies has been about two and a half years in recent times. With these kinds of changes along with the mergers, spin-offs and downsizing, monitoring companies for investment has become a greater challenge.

This book would not be possible without help from Jilleen R. Westbrook, Ph.D. She was a key additional partner that we needed during the process of drafting and completing this book. Dr. Westbrook received her Ph.D. in Economics from The Claremont Graduate University in 1993 and spent the years 1993 through 2000 working as a professor at Temple University, University of Southern California and Claremont McKenna College, teaching economics and finance. She has been invaluable in writing, organizing and editing this book. She researched our investment concepts, assuring that we are based on sound documented investment theory. She wrote chapter drafts based upon our ideas and urged us to complete drafts when we were busy on the road. Jilleen also created our Web site that provides sector and industry relative strength charts not readily available to most brokers. The few firms that do provide consistent relative strength research do not broadly distribute it to retail clients and financial advisors. We found that there was a need for relative strength information that was easy to use by both brokers and investors.

We are also grateful to Sheryl MacPhee for the excellent design, layout and typesetting of this book and to Kelly Halloran for data input and Web site updates.

In the next chapters, we will show you how using investment research effectively can help you to survive the massive amount of seemingly useless research available from investment houses, research boutiques, on-line sources, and from the media, and create a winning portfolio. Our intended audience for this book is both financial advisors and serious investors. Most investors will find that while they can manage their own portfolios using this book as guidance, they will not want to. Our experience shows that the best investment portfolios are a result of discipline and effective management, and that it takes the team of advisor and investor to yield the best results.

Rod Hagenbuch
Richard Capalbo

CHAPTER 1

The Democratization of Wall Street

How Technology and an Educated Population
Have Changed the Business of Investing

During the past 10 years, the number of people directly owning stocks has grown dramatically. Americans now have more money in securities than they have in bank accounts. At least 100 million Americans — the highest percentage of the population in history — own securities directly or in mutual funds.[1] An aging population and a lack of faith in government-sponsored retirement benefits are but a couple of changes that have spurred the desire to secure a safe retirement and legacy. The economic growth of the late 20th century allowed a greater percentage of the population to acquire wealth, and as a result, an interest in investing. We shouldn't underestimate the importance of the bull market of the 1980s and 1990s in motivating individuals to save and invest as well.

Because of the growth of stock ownership, the demand for good information about securities is substantial. In keeping with the American traditions of thrift, industry, education and equality, it's not surprising that investors want to do for themselves what they once could not – namely execute effective stock trades and manage their money successfully. The information age has made it possible for investors to access enormous resources that support good investing. They use the Internet for research and lower cost executions on their stock transactions. During the market corrections of the late 20th century and early 21st century, investors increasingly began to question the wisdom of the do-it-yourself approach.

The new market for investment information has grown so vast that it is now very difficult to sort through all of the information available. Investors often misunderstand and misapply the given information, especially when market activity is very volatile. Too much of the information available fails to provide guidance about how to construct a diversified portfolio of stocks. Without diversifying, investors are exposed to unnecessary risks. Nonetheless, investors are investing more and more without the help of a traditional stockbroker. Instead of hearing "My broker suggested that I purchase shares in XYZ Corporation," you hear, "I read on the Internet that XYZ Corporation is a great stock."

The growth of information is a double-edged sword. On the one hand, an investor has access to more research than has ever before been available. On the other hand, there is so much information he cannot possibly process it all. Investors need a method to screen the information for the nuggets. How does one sort through the information that is available electronically, on television programs and in magazines? A trip to the local bookstore can yield a stack of magazines on the subject that is too heavy to carry. Names like <u>Forbes</u>, <u>Worth</u>, <u>Barron's</u>, <u>Kiplinger's</u>, and <u>Money</u> are but a few on the shelves, not to mention the large sections that hold many excellent books on the topic. In the past, business sections of metropolitan newspapers reported financial market news. These same newspapers are now sponsoring major events. Star power investment programs featuring discount and online brokers are available as those brokers position themselves as a major source of investment information. Brokers now feature investment experts on their Web sites, much like business magazines have traditionally done. How is an investor supposed to find the nuggets?

The average investor is becoming increasingly sophisticated in his use of information — demanding relevant reports about company policies, revenues, earnings and product development — but he often lacks the tools and knowledge with which to discern what is needed and then to organize information effectively. Many investors fail to use an overall strategy, or they create a flawed strategy when organizing their portfolios, exposing themselves to tremendous risks with an unbalanced portfolio. The focus on much of the investment information in the public domain is primarily on the stories surrounding individual companies' stocks. Because of the "news bite" orientation of broadcast news, and the focus upon information from stock analysts in most publications, few of these sources provide comprehensive, strategy-oriented information that integrates companies, industries, sectors, macro-economic and market trends. Most of this information is useless for long-term investment purposes. *Only by using a comprehensive set of information sources can investors manage risk and achieve their goals.* Not having a comprehensive approach to investing would be similar to a medical specialist working without a team. The specialist can't meet all of a patient's comprehensive needs, in the same way that a stock analyst only provides information about his particular industry.

Information that provides a **framework or platform** for investing and making portfolio choices is difficult to find in an organized manner from free public sources. One of the major problems is that many Web sites and magazines provide excellent information about stock prices, and recommend that readers purchase certain stocks, but they fail to link their recommendations to information on market movements in the macro-economy. An investor might read a great story about an excellent company in a magazine, but if he buys stock in that company, and is unaware that the industry is out of favor in the market, even if the company is the best in its industry, he will likely have made a bad investment decision. A common result from making investment decisions without a framework or platform is that investors choose stocks that under-perform the market, simply because they don't know that a particular economic sector is expected to be hurt by a government policy, an economic trend, or that market sentiment is against that stock's particular sector. This book is designed to provide a framework for investing to help investors organize information, identify the "nuggets," and create a diversified portfolio of stocks.

The Democratization of Wall Street

Some History: The Democratization of Wall Street

Perhaps a little historical perspective on information and changes in Wall Street is needed at this point. In the early 1970s, a small west coast firm named Mitchum, Jones, and Templeton used a technicality of the Pacific Stock Exchange to provide deep discounts on institutional orders in the equity market. This discounting business was very successful, but most of Wall Street ignored this success and the individuals who were slowly changing the securities business. The private network of Wall Street managers didn't pay much attention to new firms. The market was protected by government regulation. Discounters were seen as the enemy, and they were not to be trusted.

One of the main reasons why the discounting business didn't grow more quickly was that Wall Street had a monopoly on information at the time. The Wall Street firms provided timely information to the public, but only through brokers. If you didn't use a Wall Street broker, you had to rely on the <u>Wall Street Journal</u> that provided yesterday's market news. An individual couldn't subscribe to <u>Business Week</u> unless he could prove that he was a worthy businessman. Most people found financial information very confusing. Wall Street did its best to maintain mysterious pricing practices and order execution systems. Prospectuses were unintelligible, and there was a huge hocus-pocus associated with the language of order entry. Since that time, prospectuses have been simplified. Most people are now familiar with some of the order entry language — limit orders, market orders, stop-loss orders, all or none, short sales, puts, calls, spreads, straddles and more. Understanding a financial report was beyond most people's capabilities. If Wall Street had not monopolized financial information, the trend toward discount brokerages would have developed much more quickly.

In spite of the problems around information dissemination, discounters were slowly able to make advances for a couple of reasons. The first was that Wall Street firms had very expensive distribution systems in place. Insiders were afraid to cannibalize their profits, because they had to maintain these costly systems. If a Wall Street firm provided a deep discount product side-by-side with their more traditional product, their brokers would have faced lost income. The fear was that brokers would walk across the street to another firm, so management was very reluctant to disrupt the status quo.

The second reason was that the back offices of securities' firms were incredibly antiquated, maintaining their "main frame"-based systems. Securities firms were handicapped and almost held hostage by their information departments. The account numbering systems were obsolete, and there was too much interdependence across operating systems. They needed personal computers (PCs)! What complicated solving the Wall Street computing problem was that management didn't know much about computers. The systems departments maintained control because of this ignorance. On the other hand, the new "discounters" were starting their firms from scratch with PC-based systems. They were able to build up-to-date systems that managed data much more effectively. On Wall Street, the "main-frame" systems couldn't process orders in great volume. For a period of time "The Street" had to close on Wednesdays in order to process volume as low as 10 million shares. The transfer of ownership was still represented by paper stock and bond certificates. We registered securities in both the names of the nominee and actual owner. Every transaction involved both the physical stock certificate and the transfer information. When the exchanges and transfer agents converted from all paper to primarily electronic records and securities transfer, the log jam was broken, and the discounters who were much more efficient with technology gained a significant advantage in cost and efficiency.

To make matters worse, the traditional way to sell securities involved paying a broker a fee for each transaction he generated. The accounting problems that went along with this type of system were great. The discounters generated many of their new accounts from advertising rather than by using an expensive distribution system of financial advisors to bring in new accounts. This way, they could control new account acquisition costs.

Not surprisingly, market forces did their work over time. Discounters made inroads, slowly but surely. The growth in personal income during the 1980s and 1990s contributed to the number of participants in the market. In the past, only a select group of wealthy individuals had a broker, because only that select group had enough money to invest. The status quo was changing. More people were getting richer, and many began to see stock market participation as key to wealth. By 1992, income distribution in the United States was its most unequal in recorded history, with much of the newly-acquired wealth linked to the performance of the stock market. Add to these trends the movement from traditional company pension plans to tax-deferred vehicles, and the preferential tax treatment stocks had over other savings vehicles, and it is not hard to understand why individuals began to demand information about the stock market. If you consider the spectacular increase in college education in America, you can see that investors are smarter and more motivated than ever to invest in the stock market.

If you go to the bookstore today, have a look at how many book titles deal with investing. Look at the newsstand and count the number of magazines on the subject of investing. Look at the expanded business sections of many of the nation's newspapers, and if you really have time, check out the Internet as a source of information on the subject of money management. If you want to know about anything from initial public offerings (IPOs) to credit to mutual funds to market research, it is all there. The Internet provides almost unlimited information and is very attractive to people. More people than ever are trading online. The world has certainly changed.

Does Anyone Still Need a Full-Service Broker?

The role of the full-service brokerage firm, and its brokers, is to organize information for clients and to provide an excellent process for stock selection. When an investor's emotions cause them to make poor choices, full-service advisors must stop them from acting on these emotions. A common mistake is recommending and choosing stocks in a haphazard manner. Without proper training, brokers have the same problems processing and organizing information as do investors. When asked to do an analysis of a client's portfolio, inexperienced advisors undertake an analysis of the individual stocks in the portfolio without thinking about how the portfolio aligns with the market, or whether the stocks are in favorable industries. In order to add value to an investor's portfolio, a broker needs to organize and provide information that is difficult to acquire and interpret. The information provided must clearly enhance the performance of the investor's portfolios, or the full-service broker will lose business to Internet and discount brokers. In this day and age, investors will not pay a premium price for execution or investment advice unless the broker and his firm enhance portfolio performance and manage risk.

The Growth of On-Line Brokerage Accounts

According to the Web site "Virtual Wall Street" (*www.virtualwallstreet.com*), in 1999 approximately 40 percent of all equity orders were placed through discounters and online brokerage houses. Charles Schwab, a leading Internet brokerage firm, indicated that 80 percent of its stock trades came in online in 2000. Even in the slump of 2001, Schwab added 600,000 active customers, even though they traded less often than during the bubble of the late 1990s. Overall in 2001, there were more than 20 million online brokerage accounts, up from 1.5 million in 1996, according to Gomez Advisors, an Internet consulting firm in Lincoln, Massachusetts. The number of Internet brokerage accounts is expected to be over 50 million by 2004, according to Forrester Research in Cambridge, Massachusetts.

Historically, full-service brokerage firms provided most of the research and financial information available in the market. What was true historically is not the case today. Brokerage houses do not have a monopoly on information any longer. Large numbers of investors search the Web for research, information news and financial services. A simple search on Yahoo's search engine yielded hundreds of sources of information about investments. The public can find statistical data on more Internet sites than the home page has room to bookmark. Online brokers provide clients with real time quotes, and vast quantities of data and research.

While full-service brokers no longer control information, they do have access to certain types of information that, if used properly, give them an advantage in helping clients. Brokers should have a system in place to discuss the "big picture" with their clients. With the use of securities research, brokers are able to create a context for investing in a particular stock, based upon economic trends, industry trends, company trends and market sentiment. Large brokerage houses have well-educated, skilled strategists and analysts whose job it is to identify trends, interpret data and access corporate leaders. A broker, if he understands how to use the information readily available to him, can easily help clients make better decisions about investing. A good broker has a comparative advantage in organizing information for investors, since he specializes in this line of work and spends his days examining research about markets and companies. While it is not impossible for the average investor to do this himself, there is a good reason not to. This point is best understood by example. Think about the most skilled surgeon in the world who is also the fastest typist in the world. Should he do his own typing? The answer is "no!" The surgeon's time is better spent specializing in surgery, because he has a comparative advantage in surgery. If he does his own typing, he is not doing surgery, and the cost of income he fails to earn while he is typing is too high. He could hire several typists to do his typing and still come out ahead by spending his time in the operating room. In the same manner, most investors do better by spending time at their chosen professions, and hiring a broker to organize investment information for them. This is not to say that investors should be uninformed. This book is intended to inform investors so that they can work more effectively with brokers.

The best full-service brokers increase investors' returns, while reducing the risks associated with their existing portfolios. In fact, one large brokerage firm (in an internal study) analyzed the portfolio performance of its clients, and found that professionally-managed portfolios "out-performed" other types of portfolio management. In their study, professionally-managed mutual funds had the second highest performance, followed by client-managed accounts where the client followed broker advice, and then client-managed accounts where the client and broker made joint decisions. The lowest performing accounts were client-managed accounts where clients made their own decisions. Good brokers talk clients out of bad decisions, and keep them in the market when downturns occur. Our experience has shown us that methods to organize information add value when well executed. Good brokers provide focused, well-organized investment information, with

13

a little wisdom, experience and common sense thrown-in. A clearly-defined process for reviewing research information improves decision-making. This book is designed to help both brokers and investors develop a framework for organizing market research and information that is logical, disciplined and that will improve portfolio performance.

CHAPTER 2

Diversification, Asset Allocation and Risk

Crucial Terminology for Investors Before Portfolio Construction

The world of finance and economics contains more jargon than most of us can manage. But in order to better understand investing, we have to talk about the assorted jargon surrounding portfolio management. Portfolio management concerns itself with the relationship between returns and risk. In this chapter, we will introduce and explain several terms that are thrown around casually in the finance industry, but that are often misunderstood. The concepts of asset allocation, diversification, and risk are important to demystify. They may sound complicated, but are really very intuitive. Once these terms are understood, discussions about investments are much more straightforward.

The most basic idea in portfolio theory is that holding all of your resources in a single asset is a very risky proposition. The old adage, "Don't put all of your eggs in one basket" is very clear; holding most of your financial resources in a single stock or a piece of real estate can damage your financial health if the company suddenly falls on bad times or the real estate market plunges. The farmer's wife knew that she should have several baskets for collecting eggs, so that if she tripped on the way back to the kitchen, there would still be eggs for breakfast.

In the world of investing, spreading your wealth across various assets works to diversify the specific risks associated each kind of asset. You can't rid yourself of all risk, but you can limit the risk associated with a particular company by holding many stocks. Market risk is the risk that comes from major economic and market trends. You cannot diversify market risk by holding long positions in many stocks. With more complicated forms of hedging strategies, you can remove market risk from a portfolio, but you expose yourself to the risks associated with a particular manager and his abilities. In all of these cases, diversification acts to manage risk.

Certain assets are very sensitive to interest rate movements, while others are less so. For example, the real estate market is highly sensitive to interest rate changes. In the early 1980s, interest rates rose to the double-digits in the United States, and the real estate market ground to a halt. When interest rates slowly began to decline, real estate picked-up again. The overall economic health of the early 1980s was reflected in the stock and the bond markets as well, because economic risk is unavoidable. However, the individual who really suffered during that time period had most of his portfolio in commercial real estate, especially when compared to an individual who had a more diversified portfolio of stocks, bonds, cash, fine art and real estate.

What is Risk?

Risk refers to how certain you are that any investment you make – be it in stocks, bonds, cash, real estate, or fine art – will produce the returns that you expect over a specific time period. There are a variety of reasons why you might not earn the desired returns. One is that the asset class has a history of producing very volatile returns. For example, the average, or mean, return for the S & P 500 index was 12.45 percent between 1990 and 2001, but the standard deviation for the S & P 500 was 12.97 over the same time period. The standard deviation is a way to measure volatility across yearly returns. Applying a little basic statistics to these numbers and forecasting into the future, we conclude that 95 percent of the time, your annual return on the S & P 500 would be between –13.49 and 38.39 percent.[1] That is quite a bit of variability on an annual basis. Recall that over the 10-year horizon, the average annual return was 12.45 percent, pointing to another source of risk, namely the time period over which you hold an asset. The longer the time period you hold stocks, the more likely you are to earn a positive return. Another reason for lower returns is because of high fees associated with very high portfolio turnover.

You can have much more volatile returns on your investments if you have a poorly-constructed portfolio. Your portfolio might substantially under-perform or out-perform the market because of the composition of stocks,

17

bonds, and cash in the portfolio, or because your stock or bond portfolio is weighted differently from a market benchmark for stocks or bonds. Because different asset classes have different risk/return characteristics, investors should understand the basic characteristics of each asset class prior to making investment decisions. If not, they may earn returns that they didn't expect because they had unrealistic expectations.

One of the most common reasons why equity portfolios fail to earn expected returns is that they are structured poorly, and deviate substantially from the market benchmark. As a portfolio diverges from its benchmark, it may be excessively risky. While high concentrations in specific areas of the market can produce significantly better returns than the benchmark, they can also result in extreme losses. The desire to earn excess returns by taking risky positions is at the heart of all financial management. Managers search for excess returns through superior stock picking and other techniques. Portfolio managers refer to excess returns as *alpha*. Managing the relationship between the search for alpha and its associated risks is one of the main topics of this book. When this process is mis-managed, potential losses are great. The risk associated with potentially high returns is seldom worth 70 to 90 percent losses or even bankruptcy, as happened when the technology sector crash began in 1999.

The Alphas and Betas of Investing

The capital asset pricing model (CAPM), a basic model in portfolio theory, explains the relationship between the returns on a stock or stock portfolio, and the returns on the market or market benchmark. The model shows that we can explain a particular portfolio's returns in light of its past performance relative to its stated benchmark with a simple equation:

$$\mathbf{R_{Pt}} = \alpha + \beta(\mathbf{R_{Bt}}) + \varepsilon_t$$

Where:

$\mathbf{R_{Pt}}$ is the return on the individual portfolio over time,

$\mathbf{R_{Bt}}$ is the return on the benchmark portfolio over time,

β is the percentage change in the individual portfolio per percentage change in the benchmark portfolio,

α is the risk adjusted excess return on the individual portfolio, and

ε_t is the error term over time.

For example, if an investor chooses a risk characteristic of her portfolio to be twice as risky as the benchmark, she will construct a portfolio with a β equal to two. If the benchmark appreciates by three percent, the investor would expect her portfolio to appreciate by six percent. If the investor earned an eight percent return, the extra two percent would be called α, alpha, or excess returns. If the market depreciated by three percent, the portfolio would be expected to depreciate by six percent. The portfolio could still earn alpha by losing only four percent. On the other hand, alpha can be negative. Some portfolios will have negative alphas. In the example above, if the alpha is negative two, the return in the up market would be only four percent, and in the down market it would be eight percent. Alpha is risk adjusted excess returns or losses, and is associated with the skill of the portfolio manager.

While we will discuss many sources of risk in this book, the main risk that we will focus upon is the risk that comes from deviations from a portfolio benchmark in the search for excess returns. The benchmark we will use in this book for a stock portfolio is the S & P 500 index. It comprises a large proportion of the world stock market capitalization, is easy to follow, and is well accepted as a benchmark.[2] If you place assets in the stock market, you should monitor how closely your stock portfolio tracks the market benchmark. The more the portfolio differs from the benchmark, the more risky it is. The S & P 500 index is widely used, but if the policy for a portfolio indicates, there are other benchmarks. Some commonly used benchmarks are the Russell 2000, the Wilshire 5000, the MSCI EAFE, which is an international index, or the S & P/Barra 500 Growth or Value indices.

Although stocks are risky as an asset class, we believe that long-term investors are better served by maintaining a large portion of their investments in the stock market. Stock portfolios have more volatility and potentially negative nominal returns and thus investors tend to be compensated for that risk. Because stocks earn high nominal returns over time, they provide a good hedge against another type of risk — inflation risk. Inflation deteriorates the buying power of money earned in the future. While we are currently living in a time period of relatively low and predictable inflation, there always remains a possibility of inflation rearing its ugly head. Stocks tend to produce higher real, or inflation-adjusted returns.

Finally, it may seem obvious, but still important to repeat that there is risk associated with any investment. There will always be unavoidable, non-diversifiable risks that comes with management style and skills, and with economic downturns or shocks, such as the crash in October 1987, the 1992 major decline, as well as the terrorist attacks of September 11, 2001.

How Does Diversification Help Minimize Risk?

Diversification refers to how you minimize risk through varying your holdings. Diversification across asset classes helps to minimize the effects of macroeconomic trends, such as falling or rising interest rates or inflation variability that tend to make bonds and cash more or less attractive relative to stocks. Within a long stock portfolio, diversification moves you closer toward the benchmark, and minimizes industry and company specific risk. A failure to diversify or heavily concentrate your holdings can hurt you, as it did those investors who held concentrated positions in the technology and communications industries during the late 1990s. You cannot diversify away market risk, but the risks associated with specific firms and industries tend to counteract one another as you hold a broad portfolio of stocks. The benchmark will have a broad range or stocks across industries for this reason.

For example, when diversifying a stock portfolio, an investor can hold stocks that tend to move in opposition to one another. If an investor holds stock in the transportation industry, he might also want to hold stock in the oil industry. The reason is specific shocks to the economy affect different industries differently. If crude oil and gasoline prices rise because of a protracted conflict within the Middle East, stock prices in the transportation industry will likely fall. This is because fuel costs will rise faster than the industry is able to pass the costs on in the form of high prices to consumers. The domestic oil industry will likely benefit from increases in the price of imported oil. As profitability increases, so will the price of domestic oil stocks. Thus the risks associated with a particular industry are smoothed by diversification.

What is Asset Allocation?

Asset allocation is a policy decision. It refers to the percentages of your overall portfolio you place in each asset category (for example: 65 percent stocks, 25 percent bonds, 10 percent cash). It may also refer to an overall willingness to bear risk within a particular asset category, for example an aggressive growth stock portfolio is more risky than a value portfolio. Asset allocation reflects your preferences. Thus asset allocation is the first step in portfolio construction. Asset allocation is not about timing the market. It is based upon your needs and preferences at any given time, and not upon current market conditions. There are times when the relative attractiveness of one class of assets may be such that — within a specific set of objectives and risk policy — the exposure to different categories can be adjusted. When interest rates are very low or very high, the base allocation can be beneficially adjusted.

With asset allocation you must assess how much risk you are willing to bear, look at the average returns across asset classes, think about your time horizon and income needs, consider your values and interests, and then make a decision about asset weights. If you are approaching retirement and have children college age, you may want to consider a different asset allocation policy than if you are younger with small children. In general, the longer your time horizon the more you should consider heavily weighting stocks within your overall portfolio. Of course, a policy decision is always a matter of personal preference. You may be unable to bear the volatility of your stock portfolio. If so, you may want to place a larger percentage of your portfolio in bonds or real estate, but you should keep in mind another source of risk — liquidity risk. A portfolio heavy in real estate is less liquid than one more heavily weighted in stocks.

Asset allocation does not only refer to financial assets, but can refer to how an investor places resources across financial and physical assets. The pie graph in Exhibit 2-1 shows how one middle-aged investor has allocated his assets into various financial and physical assets. As he ages, he will likely alter the composition of this portfolio as a matter of policy. The portfolio weights will change over time if the portfolio is neglected. Unless all assets increase or decrease in value by the same amount, which is highly unlikely, the port-folio weights will change as asset classes yield different returns. If the stock market grows by twice the amount of the other holdings, the weight of the stock portfolio in the mix increases. The investor will not only have to assess his own changing needs and policy choices over time, but also alter the portfolio composition to bring it back into line with the appropriate allocation as the market changes it. This activity is called "rebalancing the portfolio."

Asset Allocation Choice: One Portfolio

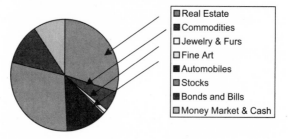

- Real Estate
- Commodities
- Jewelry & Furs
- Fine Art
- Automobiles
- Stocks
- Bonds and Bills
- Money Market & Cash

How are Financial and Physical Assets Different?
Physical assets, like real estate or jewelry, are different from financial assets. Although both types of assets are "stores of value" and can earn future returns, physical assets depre-ciate and require insurance and maintenance or development since they are being used or

worn. The purchase of physical assets does not necessarily require that the investor forgo future consumption for future earnings and the market for the exchange of physical assets is much less liquid than the market for financial assets. Most individuals do not purchase diamond rings in order to place them in a safe deposit box to keep them flawless for the purpose of future sales. People purchase diamond rings to give to their loved ones or they purchase them to wear themselves. Certainly the diamond ring maintains value, but the market for physical assets is thin and risky. Real estate is an exception to this principle. Holding undeveloped real estate as a source of future income is still a risky proposition. Land is unique in its abilities to be developed and altered over time. Real estate investments are particularly time sensitive and risky because carrying charges are significant. Carrying charges include interest expenses, property taxes, risk of zoning law changes and lack of liquidity.

Financial Assets	**Physical Assets**
Stocks	*Commodities* –
Bonds and Bills	Gold, Silver,
Mutual Funds	*Agricultural Products*
Money Market Funds	*Real Estate* –
Cash –	Commercial, Residential
Bank checking,	*Collections* – Art, Coins,
savings accounts	Jewels
	Durable Goods –
	Automobiles, Computers

Asset Allocation Over Time

If an investor neglects his portfolio over time, it can become terribly unbalanced. Let's say that an investor places $50,000 in the stock market and $50,000 in the bond market in the first year, and desires a percentage split of 50/50 as a matter of policy. Over that year, assume that the stock market appreciates by 50 percent, but that the bond market remains unchanged. Market action changes the relative values invested in the two asset classes. The portfolio weights change over the year to 60 percent, 40 percent. In the next year if the stock market corrects downward, 60 percent of the portfolio will decline rather than 50 percent. If the portfolio is not rebalanced, the portfolio will have the most risk when equity markets are at peak prices, because the price appreciation alone causes the portfolio to have "higher than policy" percentages in stocks. The opposite is also true. When the equity markets decline, the unmanaged portfolio has the smallest allocation in equities at the most attractive time to hold equities. Failing to adjust portfolios over time leads to more risky portfolios and lower market returns. Market action works across asset classes and within asset classes. If a stock portfolio is ignored, holdings in certain stocks will grow over time, and holdings in other stocks will fall. If an investor fails to rebalance his portfolio, he will often end up with a much more risky portfolio than he wants.

How do You Make a Good Asset Allocation Choice?

Some investors might find it difficult to assess how much of their portfolio they should invest in stocks versus bonds, cash and other assets. Stocks have more short-term price risk, while bonds are associated with more interest rate and inflation risk. Since we live in a world where there is a positive rate of inflation, the real or inflation corrected returns are what matter to investors. Cash holdings will tend to earn negative real returns, since the value of a fixed amount of cash erodes with inflation (see text box example). T-bills and bonds do a little better in terms of average real returns, but stocks tend to yield positive real returns over longer time horizons, as their nominal returns are high enough to offset inflation. On the other hand, stock prices, particularly global and growth stock prices, are generally more volatile than bond and T-bill prices.

T-Bill Yields: An Example

To understand risk and tax adjusted returns, the following illustration shows why short-term T-bills will never allow an investor to meet long-term goals. If T-bills are yielding three percent, an investment of $1,000 will result in a taxable income of $30 for the year. If you apply the 36 percent federal tax, plus up to 11 percent additional state taxes, the net after tax return to the investor is around $19.20. If inflation is two and a half percent, the purchasing power of the $1,019.20 at the end of the year will have depreciated by the inflation rate to $993.72 in real terms. If one invests in this manner for 20 years, the purchasing power of the original investment becomes $880. This investor will never send his kids to college or provide a reasonable retirement with this investment strategy.

> ### Asset Allocation:
> ### Types of Risk to Consider
> *Volatility or price risk* – Stock price fluc-
> tuations, or more technically the standard devi-
> ation of stock returns. Sometimes these mea-
> surements are expressed as a portfolio beta with
> an R-squared measurement to show the consis-
> tency of return.
> *Inflation risk* – The probability that the
> value of a financial asset or income declines
> as inflation reduces the purchasing power of a
> country's currency.
> *Interest rate risk* – The possibility that a
> bond or other fixed income security will decline
> in value as a result of a rise in interest rates.[3]

Once you have decided what percent of your portfolio will be allocated toward stocks, you need to decide
upon a stock portfolio style. You may choose to create
a stock portfolio that is more aggressive or highly risky.
A portfolio that is designed as an "aggressive growth"
portfolio typically has more risk associated with it than
one that is designed to be more "blue chip." Portfolios are structured to implement a strategic plan. A
more highly- risky portfolio is associated with a higher
expected return but can also face profound losses. When
designing a portfolio, an investor should have a clear
idea of the goals for the portfolio, and for his willingness
to bear risk.

Common Problems with Portfolio Construction
A common fallacy that gets investors in trouble is the

belief that if they spread money across enough assets, they will have low risk in their portfolios. A portfolio might be terribly risky within an asset class. For example, a local doctor may own his home, a commercial real estate building downtown, a large orange grove, a condominium in the mountains that is rental property, and a beach home. This is a fairly diversified real estate portfolio, but it is far from a risk-less one. Not only is the portfolio sensitive to interest rates, but also all of the properties are concentrated within a small region, subject to state policies on taxes and economic issues. If real estate is the main investment the doctor has, he is missing the opportunity for returns and risk reduction provided by other assets.

People tend to invest in assets they know, but often end up with portfolios that are too highly concentrated. We think of the jeweler who has a large portfolio of gemstones, but little else by way of investments. People do the same thing with their stock portfolios. Investors purchase stocks that they know, often resulting in highly-concentrated positions in the stock market.

There is not a single asset allocation choice that is ideal for all people, neither is there a single asset allocation choice that is ideal for one person over his entire lifetime. This policy choice has to be addressed over the phases of one's life. Each person must evaluate his tolerance for the risks associated with each type of asset. Asset allocation is a process. We advocate holding a variety of asset types in order to diversify holdings, but evidence suggests that the stock market provides the highest inflation-adjusted returns and is actually less risky than other financial markets over time horizons greater than 15 years.[4] Individuals will maximize future wealth by focusing their investments on stock market choices. If your time horizon is 15 years or longer, we recommend that you allocate most of your resources toward the stock market. Then use advice to construct a well-diversified stock portfolio that tracks your benchmark closely. Where to gain the advice about structuring a good stock portfolio is discussed in Chapters 5 through 8 of this book.

Why the Stock Market?

We focus on diversification within the stock market, because we believe that most investors are better served by focusing their investment strategies on the allocation of assets within the stock market for two reasons:

1. Allocation within the stock market is most overlooked. Too often asset allocation decisions stop after an investor decides how much money to place in stocks, bonds and cash in his 401(k).
2. In his text, <u>Stocks for the Long Run</u>, Jeremy J. Siegel, Ph.D. argues that real returns are actually less risky for stocks than they are for bonds in time horizons over 10 to 15 years.

In addition, these investments receive delayed and favorable tax treatment. By investing in the stock market, rather than the bond market or cash, inflation risk and interest risk are lowered. The main reason why you would not want to concentrate your portfolio in stocks is if you have current cash or income needs or if your time horizon is under 15 years. It makes sense for an investor to focus upon the stock market and to diversify specific risks within that asset class in order to earn the highest risk- adjusted real returns.

Remember that diversifying a long stock portfolio minimizes certain kinds of risk, but cannot eliminate market risk. The stock market has bull periods and bear periods that tend to be associated with expectations about the general health of the economy. For example, if most market participants believe that GDP (gross domestic product) will rise in the next quarter, that will be good for corporate profits on the whole, and the stock market will tend to appreciate in value. The opposite is also true. If GDP is expected to fall, the market will tend to depreciate in value. Stock returns tend to rise and fall with the market, and thus the term market risk.

On the other hand, sector, industry and firm-specific risks can be diversified. Some market sectors such as the retail sector tend to be very sensitive to economic upturns and downturns. Other sectors are less sensitive, like the utilities sector. By holding stocks in each of these sectors, investors minimize sector-specific risks. Likewise, some industries are profoundly affected by bad weather such as the foods industry, while other industries such as computer software and services are not. In financial terms, industries that move together in the face of shocks are industries that are positively correlated. If industries move in opposition to each other, they are negatively correlated. In order to reduce risk, portfolios should be constructed such that they include firms within industries that offset each other in the face of shocks or are negatively correlated. Industry strategists consider these relationships when they construct sector groups for portfolio construction.

How Should an Investor Think About Risk When Constructing a Portfolio?

When constructing a stock portfolio, the fundamental measure of risk is how far away the portfolio is from a market benchmark. Since we cannot diversify market risk, the minimal return we would seek is that of the market. The more a portfolio deviates from the market portfolio, the more risky it is. If the market benchmark is the Standard and Poor's 500 Industries (S & P 500), we want to construct a portfolio that "hugs" the market but that is constructed with a few active bets to seek alpha. If you simply want to earn the market return and don't want to bear additional risk, hold an S & P 500 Index Fund (there are some tax consequences associated with holding a mutual fund rather than a stock portfolio that we will discuss in Chapter 12). In order to earn excess returns (alpha), we need a framework to strategically pick stocks in sectors and industries that are expected to do well relative to the rest of the market. In this way we add the possibility of beating the benchmark.

There are approximately one dozen major sectors identified by Standard & Poors. Financial strategists create these sector groupings of stocks based upon how the industries and firms within each sector have behaved in the past with respect to various economic shocks and transitions. Strategists use economic theory to guide their choices regarding the creation of sector groups that are expected to respond differently during economic shocks. By holding stocks within each sector group, you act to diversify your holdings.

Different strategists group sectors slightly differently, and the sector groupings change over time as firms develop and technologies change. In other words, sector definitions are not set in stone. For example, General Electric was historically classified as an electrical equipment company. As the company changed its products, shifting from primarily electrical equipment to aircraft, finance and financial services, it recently was reassigned as a multi-industry company.

Beyond sector groups, there are around 125 industry groups from which to choose stocks. Each industry group falls into a sector or composite. For example, in one strategist's groupings, the energy sector has five industry groupings for oil & gas: 1) drilling & equipment, 2) exploration & production, 3) refining and marketing, 4) domestic integrated, and 5) international integrated. Within number "5" — international integrated — there are four companies represented in the market (S & P 500), (1) Chevron Corp., (2) Exxon Mobil Corp., (3) Royal Dutch Petroleum, and (4) Texaco Inc. By grouping these stocks in such a manner, the strategists are indicating that the five industry groups identified face slightly different risk factors, and the stock prices of the firms within one industry group have behaved similarly in the past in response to markets news and economic shocks.

Investment strategists organize market data and construct portfolios based upon sectors and industry groupings. In each portfolio a sector of the market comprises a percentage of the market capitalization. The percentage of the market capitalization that a sector or industry group holds is its weight in the portfolio. If a portfolio is in balance with regard to sector percentages, we diversify price/volatility risk. By holding a sector neutral portfolio we eliminate benchmark-tracking risk, and we potentially earn alpha through superior stock selection. The more a portfolio deviates from "the market" portfolio with respect to sector and industry weights, the greater the risk associated with the portfolio.

Investment strategists try to improve portfolio performance relative to the market by over-weighting or under-weighting different sectors and industries based upon their firms' analyses. Strategists identify the most/least attractive sectors and industries in the market by analyzing economic forecasts and trends. By following their recommendations, investors can earn excess returns if their over-weighted sectors out-perform the market, or if their under-weighted sectors under-perform the market.

Conclusion

The relationship between risk and returns is positive on average over time. The more a portfolio deviates from its benchmark, the more potential gains and potential losses. Understand the nature of the risks you take when you construct your portfolio of financial assets. Re-assess at major life-turning points. If you have long-term goals, focus your efforts on constructing a stock portfolio that manages risk, but provides excellent returns. The following chapters provide a guide about how to do just that!

CHAPTER 3

Building Stock Portfolios vs. Picking Stocks

Discovering Why "The Big Picture" is Essential for Successful Securities Research

Stock selection should be part of building a portfolio. Investors need a process that supports the selection of good stocks for a portfolio. A common but potentially costly mistake occurs when investors construct portfolios without considering the *portfolios*. The mistake happens easily enough when investors choose attractive individual stocks without an overall investment processes. This practice can come to resemble a dinner party where the hostess serves only rice: jasmine, basmati, short grained, wild and so on. The dinner is diverse in terms of rice offerings, but it isn't well balanced and doesn't achieve the desired results — namely satisfied and happy guests. A well-designed set of investment criteria and a structured investment process help to build a (balanced) portfolio. Stock "picking" is very important, but is not the first step in the process of building a portfolio. Creating a process that filters, organizes and structures information must come first. The second step establishes income, risk and growth goals for the portfolio. The third step involves layers of research to identify excellent sectors and industries of the economy for investing. Finally at the end of the process, stock selection begins.

The early 21st century served as a painful reminder to investors about why risk management and balanced investment portfolios are important. Individual stock selection — without putting each stock into the bigger portfolio picture — can result in a very risky business. A lack of proper diversification and heavily over-weighted industry sectors can lead to huge losses. A good example of this problem was the mid-1990s' rapid price appreciation of "tech stocks" such as Intel and Cisco. Holding such stocks without the benefit of a more balanced portfolio led to huge losses for investors in 1999 through 2001. The same mistakes were made with managed accounts and mutual funds. Holding a technology sector fund or an Internet fund in addition to these stocks just compounded the risk, and the subsequent punitive price declines.

When we argue for a portfolio approach to choosing stocks, we are suggesting that investors first look at recommendations regarding sector and industry allocations within a portfolio and then choose stocks to fit the portfolio needs. The portfolio comes first. On the other hand, a common approach to portfolio construction involves picking stocks based upon tips and recommendations from trusted sources. We call this the "hot stock tip" approach to portfolio construction. If an investor takes this approach, he may end up with a very unbalanced portfolio and exposed to excess risk.

We provide several examples that show the results of the "hot stock" approach to portfolio construction and the potential pitfalls. The first is based upon a Kiplinger's magazine cover article from their January 2001 edition that read, "The 10 Stocks to own in 2001…you'll lasso big bucks in the year ahead." Exhibit 3-1 shows the 10 recommended stocks from that article. Suppose a college graduate, with graduation money in hand, read the Kiplinger's article and purchased those 10 stocks for his portfolio, based upon Kiplinger's recommendation. Exhibit 3-2 provides an analysis of the "10 stock" portfolio relative to the market.

Exhibit 3-1
Ten Stocks to Own in 2001

Company	Ticker
Pepsico	PEP
Tyco International	TYC
Carnival Corp.	CCL
Clear Channel Communications	CCU
Nortel Networks	NT
Parker Hannifin	PH
El Paso Energy	EPN
Lowe's	LOW
FileNet	FILE
Southwest Airlines	LUV

source: Kiplinger's, January 2001, pp. 40-44

Exhibit 3-2 includes two columns titled "Portfolio Percent" and "S & P Percent." These weights represent the percent of the overall portfolio held in each stock, where the overall S & P portfolio is the S & P 500 index. We "purchased" equal values or weights of each stock in the portfolio, because the magazine didn't suggest any weighting scheme to the purchases. The exhibit also provides information on basic indicators of the portfolio such as price/earnings ratios relative to the S & P 500 (see text box on following page). For example, the price/earnings ratio for the portfolio analyzed in Exhibit 3-2 is 3.26 times greater than the S and P average.

Table 3-2
Ten Stocks to Own

Sectors	Portfolio Percent	S&P Percent
Utilities	0	3.17
Energy	10	7.21
Financials	0	17.83
Industrial Cyclicals	20	11.38
Consumer Durables	0	1.54
Consumer Staples	10	7.87
Services	30	11.18
Retail	10	6.74
Health	0	14.78
Technology	20	18.27
Not Available	0	0.05

Indicator	Portfolio	Relative to S&P
P/E Ratio	98.78	3.26
P/B Ratio	3.64	0.64
ROA	4.98	0.54
3 Year Earnings Growth %	25.17	1.58
Yield %	1.14	0.95

As you can see, there are several important sectors that are not represented in this portfolio. The financial sector that comprises 17.83 percent of the S & P 500 and the health care sector that comprises 14.78 percent of the S & P 500 are both severely under-weighted, with no stocks representing those sectors in the portfolio. On the other hand, the consumer staples sector is severely over-weighted relative to the overall market. While Kiplinger's did not recommend that the investor hold only these stocks, they did focus upon the stocks and *not* on how they fit in a portfolio. One might argue that most sophisticated investors wouldn't make the mistake of holding only 10 stocks. While we admit that this is an extreme example, it is quite telling. Major sectors are not represented in the portfolio, which is a fairly common mistake. The portfolio is out-of-balance, thus creating unnecessary risk, and at a potentially significant cost.

Price/Earning Ratio (P/E)

One of the primary measures of a stock's relative value is its P/E. Because companies are growing at different rates, and the price of a company's stock represents market expectations regarding the future earnings, P/E ratios vary widely. P/E ratios are normally expressed in terms of the current earnings. Some companies sell for three to five times earnings, and others sell at very high stock prices even when the company is experiencing substantial current losses. In each case, the P/E ratio reflects future expectations. When a P/E is very low, inves-

---

tors' expectations regarding future earnings are low. In most cases they expect earnings to decline or for the company to experience losses in the future. When P/E ratios are very high, investors expect significant growth in the future and see the future for the company as being very positive.

How does an investor decide if a P/E ratio is too low, too high, or just right? It is important to keep in mind that indicators such as P/E ratios are not scientific. One cannot ascertain with any degree of certainty what a good P/E ratio is. However, there is an art to using P/E ratios. One particularly good artist was Peter Lynch of Fidelity Investments. He created his own ratio that some find to be a particularly useful measurement.

Price/Earnings/Growth Rate Ratio (PEG)

This measurement was first popularized by Peter Lynch and is sometimes called the Lynch ratio. The PEG is the P/E divided by the expected growth rate of the company. If a company is selling at a current P/E ratio of 10 and is expected to grow at 10 percent a year in the future, the PEG is one. If the current P/E ratio is 30 and the earnings are expected to grow at 15 percent per year, the PEG is two. Generally the closer the PEG ratio is to one, the more appropriately priced the stock. The PEG ratio is a useful tool for stock valuations, but is only one of many considerations an investor should use.

Price to Book (P/B)

The price to book ratio is relevant when a company's assets are important to the company's value. This measure is particularly troubling given the current issues surrounding questionable accounting practices.

Return on Assets (ROA)

Return on assets provides a measure of the relationship between profitability and the current assets owned by the firm.

Some investors object to portfolios with too many small stocks. The "Top 10" portfolio had several small companies represented, and one might argue including small companies in the portfolio caused the imbalance in the portfolio. A different approach to stock selection often used by investors involves choosing "big names." Stocks with well-known products and large market capitalizations often are considered safe and secure. We took the top 20 companies (based upon market capitalization) of 1997 and placed them in an equally-weighted portfolio for analysis. This particular investment philosophy leads to certain kinds of risks and returns. Exhibit 3-3 provides an example of the top 20 stocks in terms of market capitalization from the year 1997. Exhibit 3-4 gives the analysis of this portfolio.

Exhibit 3-3
Top 20 Companies of 1997

Capitalization	Ticker	% Market
General Electric	GE	3.03
Exxon	XOM	2.72
Coca-Cola	KO	2.58
Microsoft	MSFT	2.22
Intel	INTC	2.07
Merck	MRK	1.72
Phillip Morris	MO	1.62
Royal Dutch	RD	1.59
Proctor & Gamble	PG	1.42
IBM	IBM	1.37
Johnson & Johnson	JNJ	1.28
Bristol-Myers	BMY	1.06
Wal-Mart	WMT	1.05
Pfizer	PFE	1.00
AIG	AIG	0.96
DuPont	DD	0.96
PepsiCo	PEP	0.90
Disney	DIS	0.88
Hewlett Packard	HWP	0.87
Citicorp	C	0.86

source: Siegel p. 64

The portfolio balance looks better than the "Top 10." There are only two sectors that are not represented in the portfolio, the utilities and the consumer durables, both of which have small weights in the S & P 500. If you look closely you'll see that this portfolio grossly over-weights the consumer staples sector, and makes active bets in the other sectors. What this portfolio shows us is that even if we choose a portfolio of large, big name companies, we can still have a portfolio that is out-of-balance and thus risky relative to the market. Notice that the portfolio is over-weighted in energy, consumer staples, healthcare and technology. By holding this portfolio, you make active bets that those sectors will out-perform the rest of the market. The portfolio is under-weighted in the financial, industrial cyclicals, services and retail sectors. It is a good idea to understand that you are making bets if you are doing so. Understanding the nature of the risk you are holding is crucial to long-term investing success.

Exhibit 3-4
Top 20 Companies of 1997

Sectors	Portfolio Percent	S&P Percent
Utilities	0	3.17
Energy	10	7.21
Financials	10	17.83
Industrial Cyclicals	10	11.38
Consumer Durables	0	1.54
Consumer Staples	20	7.87
Services	5	11.18
Retail	5	6.74
Health	20	14.78
Technology	20	18.27
Not Available	0	0.05

Indicator	Portfolio	Relative to S&P
P/E Ratio	36.08	1.19
P/B Ratio	6.54	1.15
ROA	8.86	0.96
3 Year Earnings Growth %	10.38	0.65
Yield %	1.59	1.32

Business Week magazine regularly recommends a portfolio of 50 stocks in its "Business Week Investor" section. Exhibit 3-5 provides an example of this portfolio from the December 18, 2001 edition, and Exhibit 3-6 provides the analysis of this portfolio relative to the market.

Exhibit 3-5
Business Week 50

Company	Ticker
Microsoft	MSFT
Time Warner	TWTC
Cisco Systems	CSCO
Oracle	ORCL
EMC	EMC
Citrix Systems	CTXS
Morgan Stanley Dean Witter	MWD
Gap	GPS
Lucent Technologies	LU
Comverse Technologies	CMVT
Sun Microsystems	SUNW
Biogen	BGEN
Charles Schwab	SC
Home Depot	HD
Dell Computer	DELL
Tellabs	TLAB
Network Appliance	NTAP
Medtronic	MDT
Amgen	AMGN
Compuware	CPWR
Applied Materials	AMAT
Tyco International	TYC
Computer Associates	CA
Best Buy	BBY
Qualcomm	QCOM
Intel	INTC
Tribune	TRB

Xilinx	XLNX
Enron	ENRNQ
Lexmark International	LXK
Omnicom Group	OMC
America Online	AOL
Guidant	GDT
MBNA	KRB
Pfizer	PFE
Solectron	SLR
Gateway	GTW
Wells Fargo	WFC
General Dynamics	GDT
Texas Instruments	TXN
Capital One Financial	COF
General Electric	GE
Kansas City Southern Industries	KSU
Wal-Mart Stores	WMT
Paccar	PCAR
Applied Biosystems+	ABI
Merck	MRK
Adobe Systems	ADBE
Reliant Energy	REI
Citigroup	C

source: <u>Business Week</u>, December 18, 2000, p. 247

You may think that a portfolio with more stocks might be more "diversified" than one with fewer stocks, but the <u>Business Week</u> portfolio shows otherwise. The "Top 20" portfolio was actually more balanced than this one. Notice the nature of the "bets" in Exhibit 3-6. Unlike the Top 20 portfolio, the consumer staples sector is not represented in the portfolio at all. On the other hand, the technology sector is over-weighted by more than double the market weight. Most of the other sectors are under-weighted. A person holding this portfolio is placing a large bet that the technology sector will out-perform the rest of the market.

Exhibit 3-6
<u>Business Week</u> 50 Portfolio

Sectors	Portfolio Percent	S&P Percent
Utilities	2	3.17
Energy	2	7.21
Financials	12	17.83
Industrial Cyclicals	10	11.38
Consumer Durables	0	1.54
Consumer Staples	0	7.87
Services	8	11.18
Retail	8	6.74
Health	12	14.78
Technology	46	18.27
Not Available	0	0.05

Indicator	Portfolio	Relative to S&P
P/E Ratio	74.19	2.45
P/B Ratio	5.55	0.98
ROA	5.9	0.64
3 Year Earnings Growth %	27.16	1.7
Yield %	3.52	2.93

The next example that we discuss is that of the typical investor who walks into a broker's office. The portfolio of stocks and the dollar amount held in each are listed in Exhibit 3-7. We provide more detail in this example about the analysis process than in earlier examples.

Exhibit 3-7
Portfolio of Typical Investor

Company	Dollar Amount
American International Group	$20,000
Morgan Stanley	$40,000
Citigroup	$50,000
Cisco System	$30,000
Microsoft	$60,000
Avon	$40,000
PepsiCo. Inc.	$50,000
Coke	$40,000
Pfizer	$70,000
General Electric	$80,000
Total Portfolio	**$480,000**

Exhibit 3-8 shows the investments, the portfolio weights broken down by sector groupings, the sector weights in the S & P 500, and an investments strategist's recommended weights for a growth/income portfolio investing style (for more on investing styles, see Chapter 4).

Exhibit 3-8
Strategist's Recommendations For Portfolios

Sector		Portfolio %	S & P	Growth/Income
Financial	$110,000	22.92%	17.70%	18.00%
American Int'l	$20,000			
Citigroup	$50,000			
Morgan Stanley	$40,000			

47

Investment Survival

Sector		Portfolio %	S & P	Growth/Income
Service	$0.00	0.00%	4.90%	11.00%
Consumer Staples	$200,000	41.67%	22.00%	22.00%
Avon	$40,000			
PepsiCo Inc.	$50,000			
Coke	$40,000			
Merck	$70,000			
Consumer	$0	0.00%	7.50%	2.00%
Cyclicals				
Technology	$90,000	18.75%	22.20%	15.00%
Cisco Systems	$30,000			
Microsoft	$60,000			
Capital Goods -	$80,000	16.67%	8.90%	8.00%
Industrial				
General Electric				
Energy	$0	0.00%	7.20%	12.00%
Basic Industry	$0	0.00%	2.60%	4.00%
Transportation	$0	0.00%	0.50%	1.00%
Utilities	$0	0.00%	6.30%	7.00%
Total Portfolio Value $480,000		**100.00%**		

The stocks are placed into the appropriate sectors. The first column indicates the cash amount of stock holdings in the portfolio. The second column shows the percentage of the portfolio in each sector, or the portfolio weights based upon a $480,000 portfolio. As in the earlier examples, this portfolio is out of balance and very risky, in spite of the fact that it is constructed with a group of great stocks. In some market sectors, the portfolio is twice the S & P market sector weighting, as with capital goods, industrial and consumer staples. At the same time, there is no exposure to other sectors at all. The investor should consider moving some investments to the more attractive parts of the market as suggested by the investment strategist, and building a portfolio that is more diversified and less risky relative to the market. If the investor chooses to follow the growth/income investing style, the investor may want to adopt the recommended portfolio weights suggested by the strategist.

To minimize risk, the first thing the investor must do is to move the portfolio more in the direction of the benchmark. By following the strategist's advice the investor reduces the risk of the portfolio and opens it up to additional growth potential. For example, General Electric is very over-weighted in the portfolio. Selling some General Electric stock in order to purchase stock in other sectors would be a good first step toward a more balanced portfolio. Further, the portfolio has over 40 percent of its resources in Avon, Pepsi, Merck, and Coke. These are great companies, but that entire sector represents just over 20 percent of the S & P 500. The portfolio is more than double-weighted in this sector of the market, and is thus doubly exposed to the risks associated with consumer sentiments. The strategist views the service sector very favorably (the S & P has a 4.9 percent weighting, while the strategist recommends an 11 percent weighting). The strategist also favors the energy, basic industry, and utilities sectors. He views all as areas for growth. The owner of this portfolio would do well by beginning research into stocks in those sectors.

The four portfolios discussed thus far were constructed as specific examples of pitfalls that occur when one focuses on stock selection before considering the goals of the portfolio. In the first three, we equally weighted each stock for simplicity. The following portfolio is an actual portfolio managed by a professional. The top 10 holdings in this portfolio represent 64.98 percent of the valuation. We list those holdings and their associated weights. Exhibit 3-9 shows the holdings in the one manager's portfolio; Exhibit 3-10 provides the analysis.

Exhibit 3-9
Professionally-Managed Portfolio

Company	% of Portfolio Assets
Pfizer	16.49
Tyco International	8.58
EMC	6.24
AOL Time Warner	5.95
Cisco Systems	5.61
Pharmacia	4.9
Citigroup	4.85
Guidant	4.67
Home Depot	4.34
American Express	3.35
Percentage of Total Portfolio in Top 10 Holdings	**64.98%**

Xilinx Inc.
Sun Microsystems
Tellabs Inc.
Texas Instruments
Univision Communications
Veritas Software
Viacom Inc.
Wal-Mart Stores
PMC Sierra Inc
Siebel Sys. Inc.
Solectron
McData Corp.

Maxim Integrated Products
Medtronic Inc.
Merck & Co Inc.
Nortel Networks Corp.
Nokia Corp.
Oracle Corp.
Enron Corp.
Flextronics Intl. Ltd
Guidant Corp.
Genentech Inc.
JDS Uniphase Corp.
Brocade Communications Systems
Burlington Resources Inc.
Ciena Corp.
Corning Inc.
Exodus Communications
Applied Micro Circuits
Allegiance Telecom Inc.
Analog Devices
Anadarko Petroleum Corp.
Bea Systems Inc.

Exhibit 3-10
Professionally-Managed Portfolio
Analysis

Sectors	Portfolio Percent	S&P Percent
Utilities	0	3.17
Energy	4.4	7.21
Financials	8.2	17.83
Industrial Cyclicals	9.9	11.38
Consumer Durables	0	1.54
Consumer Staples	0	7.87
Services	2.57	11.18
Retail	6.29	6.74

Sectors	Portfolio Percent	S&P Percent
Health	27.52	14.76
Technology	41.12	18.27
Not Available	0	0.05

Indicator	Portfolio	Relative to S&P
P/E Ratio	105.02	3.46
P/B Ratio	6.54	1.07
ROA	8.86	0.68
3 Year Earnings Growth %	10.38	1.5
Yield %	1.59	0.37

Notice that this portfolio analysis looks similar, but not identical to the <u>Business Week</u> 50. The holder is significantly over-weighting the technology sector, but also over-weights the health sector. The rest of the sectors are slightly under-weighted. The investor is basically making bets on two sectors of the economy. The portfolio is not horribly out of balance, but there are indeed active bets. The investor structured the portfolio to look this way. The portfolio didn't evolve on its own to look this way. One thing about this portfolio that stands out is the very high price/earnings (P/E) ratio of the professionally-managed portfolio. The investor in the professionally-managed portfolio has clear, aggressive growth goals in mind.

The investor in the professionally-managed portfolio did not construct this portfolio by focusing upon "hot stock picks." He is choosing to emphasize the health care and technology sectors within a more balanced portfolio. How the investor came to emphasize those specific sectors is the subject of Chapter 5 in this book.

Having an unbalanced portfolio can be a choice, but that is exactly what it should be — a choice. Applying a "hot-stock" approach to portfolio construction will generally lead to making active bets on certain sectors of the economy, but the investor is often unclear about why he is making those bets.

We cannot emphasize enough the importance of understanding the nature of the risks in the portfolio you construct. A stock-focused approach can lead to portfolios that are very risky and out-of-balance. If you desire aggressive growth in a portfolio, make sure that you have a plan in mind and choose the sectors that strategists are earmarking for aggressive growth. If you do not have a process in place, you may desire a conservative portfolio and end up with a wildly speculative one, and vice versa.

In most of the examples provided, we used Morningstar Instant X-Ray *(www.morningstar.com)* to analyze the portfolios. If you want to analyze a portfolio, log on to the web site, input the ticker identifiers and the portfolio weights or dollar amounts invested, and hit "return." The web site does the rest!

How Did We Come to Focus Upon Stocks and Not Portfolios?

Over half of all stockbrokers and most investors have entered the market during the past 15 years. Brokerage houses have provided good training, focusing much of it on gathering assets, managed accounts and packaged products. We believe that it is time to focus much more on using investment information to create balanced portfolios.

Financial advisors must understand how to analyze

portfolio construction, and how to manage the invest-ment process. Many, if not most, individual portfolios are seriously out of balance. Many investors have several accounts. The accounts may include managed accounts, mutual funds and individual stocks, resulting in overlap or stock duplication. The client and advisor should analyze all investments to maintain a balanced total portfolio.

If one looks at market trends over the last 20 years, the bull markets of the late 20th century explain quite a lot about the state of investment education. In a bull market, even a poorly-constructed portfolio of stocks can yield positive returns. The results may be lower than the overall market portfolio, but they will be positive none-theless. Investors pay too little attention to portfolio construction and risk management when the numbers are growing! It is easy to forget about the downside when the stock market trend is forcefully positive. But times have changed.

Portfolio neglect is so common and yet so potentially disastrous to the quality of individuals' lives. Why do individuals neglect their investments? Part of the expla-nation is the bull market, but another common source of portfolio neglect occurs when an individual inherits stocks from a relative who left the portfolio unattended. There are several other reasons for poorly-constructed portfolios. A common one occurs when an individual inherits a large amount of a single stock. A single stock portfolio is very common and occurs for a variety of reasons. Often individuals sell their family businesses in exchange for stock, or receive stock from employers through stock options or company-restricted stock.

Emotional attachments to companies and tax considerations explain unbalanced portfolios. We know a woman who holds the majority of her stock portfolio in General Electric. While this stock is terrific, her portfolio is subject to the risks within the financial management and capital goods sectors. When we suggested to her that she might want to sell some of the stock and invest in other sectors of the market, she said, "Honey, General Electric has appreciated so much since I bought it, I'd have to pay a fortune in taxes!" The problem with her rationale is that she is missing growth potential in companies in other sectors, and is exposing herself to the specific company risks of General Electric and its singular management team. Between 1970 and 1990, holders of very large single-stock positions used the same logic and avoided paying taxes on their "great stocks." If those "great stocks" were Eastman Kodak, Xerox and Polaroid, they no longer have to worry about taxes — they have to worry about having no assets. Those holding Eastman Kodak, Xerox and Polaroid during the 1970 and 1980s thought they owned the likes of General Electric. We cannot emphasize enough how important it is to analyze portfolios on a regular basis and diversify.

How Does a Portfolio-Based Approach Help Save Time?

With so much information available from Web sites, magazines, newspapers and television, a portfolio orientation actually simplifies the process of selecting individual stocks and mutual funds. Sorting through every source of information is impossible without a predetermined guide. We don't want to be misled into mistakes by "trusted" sources of information. We want to be able to know every time we look at any research report or article on a stock or industry whether it is important and relevant to our investment program.

With the proper foundation and guidelines, we can stay in control of all of the information and spend time reading only selected information necessary to manage our portfolios. Ninety percent of information available is not useful to investors' needs at any specific point in time! Most information is unrelated to the current or desired composition of a portfolio. If it does not fit our "screen," it can be comfortably discarded because it is not relevant to what we are trying to do. The key is differentiating between the good information and relevant information. We want relevant information.

Conclusion

Portfolio review is a starting place. It begins to address the question that we should all ask regularly about our investments, "Where are we?" If we know where we are, we are able to understand how much risk we are assuming by holding our current investments. We are also able to identify excellent opportunities for growth with a more diversified set of stocks.

A portfolio approach has the benefits of: 1) saving the investor time by abbreviating the amount of research necessary; 2) focusing the investor upon the goals and research necessary for the portfolio; and 3) avoiding excessive and unwanted risk exposure. In this chapter we provided several examples of the pitfalls associated with a "hot stock" tip approach to investing. We hope that investors will begin to ask questions along the line of, "What sectors are you over-weighted in your portfolio?" rather than, "What stocks do you like?" While choosing good stocks is very important to the investment process, stock choice should come at the end of a well-organized, well researched process.

CHAPTER 4

Portfolio Styles

How to Determine a Benchmark Style
to Meet Your Investment Needs

Before any investor begins purchasing stocks and mutual funds, he needs to examine his investment philosophy and needs. What are the goals he has for his portfolio? How much risk is he willing to tolerate? What is his age? Does he have dependents? When he has a sense of his investing philosophy and needs, he should look to investing formats and recommendations made by investment strategists in order to identify specific portfolio styles. Ideally, a portfolio style should closely reflect his investing philosophy and needs. This chapter discusses particular portfolio styles of investment strategists, their strengths and weaknesses, and provides some examples of performance.

If we could identify *with certainty* the one sector,

industry, and stock that would out-perform all of the others during a particular time period, then it would pay to invest all of our resources in that sector, industry or stock. We wouldn't need an investment style. We would simply purchase the stock that would out-perform and be done with it. Ah, if life and investing were only so simple! Investment strategists wouldn't be necessary. In reality, their research is very helpful, because the world is uncertain. Strategists make recommendations based on forecasts. Forecasts suggest which sectors and industries will out-perform the others. When a strategist recommends over-weighting a sector, it is because he has information that leads him to believe that a sector will out-perform the market.

If we choose to over-weight or under-weight a sector or industry relative to the benchmark, we take on risk. The risk is a function of the degree to which we over/under-weight. By following the strategists' recommendations, we are choosing to "buy into" their forecasts and take on the risks that they suggest. If the recommendations are right, the investor is rewarded with excess returns (returns above the market return). If they are wrong, the investor is hurt by losses (returns below the market return).

Strategists alter their recommendations about portfolio weights based upon the objectives they have for a particular portfolio. The goal of any portfolio that is actively managed — with a particular set of objectives, or investment style — is to out-perform "the market," but with considerations for investor philosophies and styles. An investment firm and its strategists typically manage several different types of portfolios representing different risk profiles. The investor must decide how much risk he is willing to bear, and to make policy decisions regarding his portfolio's goals and objectives. The investor chooses an investment style when he constructs a particular type of portfolio. Let us be specific.

One investor may construct a *growth portfolio* in which the companies represented pay very small or no dividends. Rather, they reinvest profits back into the firm in order to facilitate more rapid future growth. Growth stocks tend to have higher price/earnings ratios, and any disappointments in earnings tend to have severe negative effects on the stock price over the short-run. If the company wisely invests its profits and the firm does indeed grow, the stock price will appreciate more rapidly than if the firm pays dividends. Typically, growth firms are relatively young, and their products and services are still developing. If an investor creates a *conservative portfolio*, she chooses stocks of companies that have mature products and services, tend to pay high dividends, are more conservatively valued and less volatile than the overall market, and expect more modest growth over time. A *value portfolio* is one in which the portfolio manager identifies strong stocks that are currently "under-priced," indicated by low price/earnings ratios relative to the market. A value portfolio can be either conservative or growth, or a combination of the two. Historically, growth portfolios have been more risky than conservative or value portfolios. There are also portfolios that are combinations of the above.

Three investing styles are seen in Exhibit 4-1: a core portfolio, a conservative portfolio, and a growth portfolio. The core portfolio combines elements of the conservative and growth portfolios. The exhibit shows side-by-side comparisons of one strategist's recommendations.

Exhibit 4-1
Strategist Weighting Recommendations
Across Portfolio Objectives

	S & P Weighting	Core	Conservative	Growth
Financials	18.0%	19.0%	20.0%	18.0%
Consumer Services	5.4%	12.0%	11.0%	14.0%
Consumer Staples	20.1%	20.0%	20.0%	18.0%
Consumer Cyclicals	7.5%	4.0%	4.0%	4.0%
Technology	22.7%	20.0%	15.0%	26.0%
Capital Goods-Industrial	8.5%	7.0%	4.0%	8.0%
Energy	7.4%	10.0%	13.0%	8.0%
Basic Industry	3.2%	3.0%	4.0%	3.0%
Transportation	0.7%	0.0%	1.0%	0.0%
Utilities	6.4%	5.0%	8.0%	1.0%

The numbers in the exhibit indicate (from left to right) the percentage of the overall market valuation held by each market sector at a point in time and the strategist's recommendations for portfolio weights for three different investing styles. Note that while the strategist emphasizes different sectors in each portfolio, the portfolios remain in relative balance with the market. By following the strategist's recommendations, an investor begins the process of managing risk by not deviating substantially from the market.

Notice that in the case of the conservative portfolio, the strategist recommends a much lower weighting in the technology and capital goods sectors, and higher weightings in the energy and utilities sectors. The conservative portfolio will normally provide a lower rate of return over a long period of time, but will be much more stable and have less risk of severe price declines. The conservative portfolio is typically comprised of larger, more stable stocks in order to reduce risk. In the growth portfolio, the strategist recommends increasing holdings in technology and services, and under-weighting energy. Over the long-term, the services and technology sectors are forecasted to grow much faster than the market, and hopefully these increased earnings will be reflected in higher prices for the stocks. In both portfolios, the strategist recommends that over 70 percent of the portfolio be placed in financials, services, consumer staples and technology, which represents 65 percent of the S & P 500 index at this time. Note that even when a strategist recommends under-weighting a particular sector, such as technology in the conservative portfolio, he still recommends that a full 15 percent of the portfolio be invested in that sector. The difference in a strategist's recommendations for the conservative and growth portfolios is explained by a trade-off between long-term growth rates and portfolio volatility.

Another way to think about portfolio construction is to consider the size of the market capitalization of the firms represented in the portfolio. Market capitalization is the value of each stock in the market at any one time. Since stock prices evolve, market capitalization does as well. In general, stocks can be categorized by market capitalization relative size as "small cap," "mid-cap," and "large-cap."

"Large cap" stocks make up the majority of the S & P 500. Broader indices, such as the Russell 2000, include "mid" to "small cap" stocks. You can create a sector-balanced portfolio, using the S & P as a benchmark, but with stocks of smaller capitalization if you desire a more aggressive portfolio style.

Historically, different time periods have been associated with more or less risk in each of these categories. For example, between 1975-1983 small stocks out-performed large stocks, and value stocks out-performed growth stocks. The oil crisis and following recession had a profound impact on oil companies that tend to be "large cap" growth firms. On the other hand, a large growth portfolio out-performed all other styles over the entire time period of 1963 through 2000. Playing the forecasting game that shifts the investor between investment styles is tough to do well. It is better to choose a style for philosophical reasons, and based upon your skills and those of your financial advisor.

There is some debate about the cut-off between capitalization categories. As of 2002, "large cap" portfolios comprise most of the S & P 500 stock index and contain firms with over $3 billion in market value. Only a few years ago, not a single firm had a $3 billion market capitalization. "Mid cap" portfolios contain firms with $750 million to $3 billion in market value, and "small cap" contain firms with $200 million to $750 million in market value. The smallest 20 percent of the market is made up of "micro cap" firms that are valued below $200 million.

Exhibit 4-2 shows long-term annual returns of stocks on the New York Stock Exchange (NYSE). The exhibit also shows the associated risks with those returns, where the firms studied are ranked by market capitalization decile from largest to smallest. Remember that market capitalization ranking is dynamic. Some of the stocks that were once "small cap" have grown into very "large cap" stocks. Good examples of this dynamic are Microsoft and Cisco.

Exhibit 4-2
Long-Term Returns of NYSE Stocks
Ranked by Size — 1926-1996

Size Decile	Compound Annual Return	Annual Risk	Type
Largest	9.84%	18.90%	Large Cap
2	11.06%	22.40%	Large Cap
3	11.49%	24.20%	Mid Cap
4	11.63%	26.70%	Mid Cap
5	12.16%	27.50%	Mid Cap
6	11.82%	28.50%	Small Cap
7	11.88%	31.00%	Small Cap
8	12.15%	34.80%	Small Cap
9	12.25%	27.30%	Micro Cap
Smallest	13.83%	46.50%	Micro Cap

Source: Siegel, p. 93

Notice that "large cap" firms tend to yield lower returns than "small cap" firms, but that the risk associated with the smaller firms is higher. Some investors are willing to bear additional risk in exchange for the higher long-run return. (See text box for more information of market capitalization and returns.)

Will Smaller Firms Grow Faster?

Between 1975 and 1983, the small cap market exploded — averaging 35.3 percent compound annual returns — more than double that of large stocks. Some of small stock premia is explained by higher transactions costs. The excess returns tend to be "streaky."

"Small stock returns tend to be highly dependent on unique economic and market circumstances" (Siegel, p. 96). There are profound January effects on small stocks.

Caveat! Don't be mistaken. Most small stocks are not growth stocks. Value stocks dominate the small stock groups. Growth stocks dominate the large cap group. Example:

The 10 Largest U.S.-Based Corporations in 1996

Growth Stocks	**Value Stocks**
General Electric	Exxon
Coca-Cola	IBM
Microsoft	
Intel	
Merck	
Phillip Morris	
Proctor and Gamble	
Wal-Mart	

Exhibit 4-3 provides examples of one large brokerage's "large cap" value and growth funds. In the two charts are the 10 largest holdings in order of the size of the holdings. Each portfolio may actually contain many more stocks, but the 10 largest holdings comprise between 35 and 45 percent of the total value of each fund. These are good examples of the types of stocks in each portfolio.

Exhibit 4-3
Example of a Value Portfolio,
Large Cap Value Fund

Company	Sector
Citigroup, Inc	Banking
SBC Communications	Telecommunications
Federal Home Loan Mortgage Corp.	Financial
Verizon Communications	Telecommunications
Phillip Morris Co.	Consumer
XL Capital	Financial
Firstenergy Corp.	Utility
Keyspan Corp.	Utility
Ambac Financial Group Inc.	Financial

Example of a Value Portfolio,
Large Cap Growth Fund

Company	Sector
General Electric	Multi-Industry
Pfizer Inc.	Health Care
Microsoft	Technology
IBM	Technology
AOL Time Warner, Inc.	Technology
Eli Lilly and Co.	Health Care
Merck & Co.	Health Care
Intel Corp.	Technology
Abbott Laboratories	Health Care
Home Depot Inc.	Consumer

One way to compare portfolio styles is with market statistics and indicators. Basic market indicators describe the differences between growth and value portfolios. Exhibit 4-4 provides a list of indicators. These are fairly standard market and stock measurement standards, and are readily available from brokers and on Web sites. What the exhibit shows is the expected. Price/Earnings (P/E) ratios are higher for growth firms than for value firms, and price to book value and past earnings per share growth tend to be higher for growth firms as well. The lower yield for the growth stocks sits in contrast to the expected earnings growth, which is much higher for a growth portfolio.

Exhibit 4-4
Standard Market Measurement Indicators

	Growth	Value
P/E to Earnings 2001	23.5	17
P/E to Earnings 2002	20.3	15
Price to Book	3.95	2
Weighted Average Yield %	1	2
5 Year EPS Growth %	24.5	11

Another good way to think about portfolio style employs the use of a grid. This method helps investors to see the blends of the various approaches to style. Recall that we introduced several possible portfolios in Chapter 3: the "Top 10" portfolio, the "Top 20 of 1997" portfolio, "The Business Week 50" portfolio and the "Profession-ally-Managed" portfolio. We have included those portfolios in this chapter, and have now included a "style" grid. Across the bottom, or horizontal axis, of the grid you will see "value, blend, growth;" and along the side, or vertical axis, of the grid you will see "large, medium, small." The horizontal axis of the grid refers to the continuum of value to growth styles, and the vertical axis refers to the size category of market capitalization that each stock fits. The numbers in the style grid represent the percentage of the portfolio in each category combination. Notice that the "Top 20 of 1997" portfolio is all "large cap" with some growth and some value. On the other hand, the "Top 10" and "Business Week 50" portfolio includes some "small cap" and "mid cap" stocks, with the "Top 10" portfolio being more heavily focused on growth stocks. The "Professionally-Managed" portfolio focuses primarily on "large cap" growth stocks, but does include some "mid cap" growth and value stocks. Each portfolio has a distinctive style blend that can be identified by the grid. The grid is useful for identifying and constructing portfolios with a specific style in mind. It is also useful for editing your stock choices if you created a portfolio very heavily weighted toward a particular style and you wanted a more balanced portfolio.

Exhibit 4-5
Ten Stocks to Own

Sectors	Portfolio Percent	S&P Percent
Utilities	0	3.17*
Energy	10	7.21
Financials	0	17.83*
Industrial Cyclicals	20	11.38
Consumer Durables	0	1.54*
Consumer Staples	10	7.87
Services	30	11.18**
Retail	10	6.74
Health	0	14.78*
Technology	20	18.27
Not Available	0	0.05
P/E Ratio	98.78	3.26
P/B Ratio	3.64	0.64
ROA	4.98	0.54
3 Year Earnings Growth %	25.17	1.58
Yield %	1.14	0.95

PORTFOLIO STYLE GRID

Value	Blend	Growth	
40%	0%	30%	Large
10%	0%	0%	Medium
0%	0%	20%	Small

Exhibit 4-6
Top 20 Companies of 1997

Sectors	Portfolio Percent	S&P Percent
Utilities	0	3.17*
Energy	10	7.21
Financials	10	17.83
Industrial Cyclicals	10	11.38
Consumer Durables	0	1.54*
Consumer Staples	20	7.87
Services	5	11.18
Retail	5	6.74
Health	20	14.78
Technology	20	18.27
Not Available	0	0.05
P/E Ratio	36.08	1.19
P/B Ratio	6.54	1.15
ROA	8.86	0.96
3 Year Earnings Growth %	10.38	0.65
Yield %	1.59	1.32

PORTFOLIO STYLE GRID

Value	Blend	Growth	
25%	5%	70%	Large
0%	0%	0%	Medium
0%	0%	0%	Small

Exhibit 4-7
<u>Business Week</u> 50 Portfolio

Sectors	Portfolio Percent	S&P Percent
Utilities	2	3.17
Energy	2	7.21
Financials	12	17.83
Industrial Cyclicals	10	11.38
Consumer Durables	0	1.54*
Consumer Staples	0	7.87*
Services	8	11.18
Retail	8	6.74
Health	12	14.78*
Technology	46	18.27**
Not Available	0	0.05
P/E Ratio	74.19	2.45
P/B Ratio	5.55	0.98
ROA	5.9	0.64
3 Year Earnings Growth %	27.16	1.7
Yield %	3.52	2.93

PORTFOLIO STYLE GRID

Value	Blend	Growth	
20%	4%	46%	Large
8%	4%	14%	Medium
2%	0%	2%	Small

Exhibit 4-8
Professionally-Managed Portfolio Analysis

Sectors	Portfolio Percent	S&P Percent
Utilities	0	3.17*
Energy	4.4	7.21
Financials	8.2	17.83
Industrial Cyclicals	9.9	11.38
Consumer Durables	0	1.54*
Consumer Staples	0	7.87
Services	2.57	11.18
Retail	6.29	6.74
Health	27.52	14.76
Technology	41.12	18.27
Not Available	0	0.05
P/E Ratio	105.02	3.46
P/B Ratio	6.54	1.07
ROA	8.86	0.68
3 Year Earnings Growth %	10.38	1.5
Yield %	1.59	0.37

PORTFOLIO STYLE GRID

Value	Blend	Growth	
24%	14%	48%	Large
6%	1%	7%	Medium
1%	0%	0%	Small

Two Investment Styles that Worked
The Dogs of the Dow

"The Dow 10 strategy, which calls for investors to buy the 10 highest yielding stocks in the Dow-Jones Industrial Average, has been regarded as one of the most successful investment strategies of all time" (Siegel, p. 65). The basic theory behind the Dow 10 strategy is "value investing." Value investors are "contrarians" that believe that the swings of optimism and pessimism about the market and individual stocks are frequently unjustified, so buying out-of-favor stocks is a winning strategy. "Since 1928, the average compound return on the Dow 10 of 13.21 percent per year has exceeded the equally-weighted Dow 30 by 1.81 percent annually, and the S & P 500 index by 2.57 percent per year over the whole period." "The standard deviation of the annual returns on the Dow 10 strategy was actually lower than the Dow 30 and only slightly more than the S & P 500 stock index." (ibid, p. 67)

The Nifty-Fifty

A group of premier growth stocks such as Xerox, IBM, Polaroid and Coca-Cola were the darlings of the institutional money managers during the early 1970s. These stocks had dividends that were good and increasing, high market capitalization, and proven growth records. Money managers suggested a policy of "buy and never sell" these "Nifty-Fifty."

Critics of this approach argued that no sizeable company could possibly be worth over 50 times normal earnings, which is what some of these firms were selling for at the time. The relation between the P/E ratios and the earnings growth of the Nifty-Fifty showed that investors traded off a higher P/E ratio (and lower current yield) for higher subsequent earnings growth.[1] Jeremy Siegel, in his book <u>Stocks for the Long Run</u>, argues "stocks with steady growth records are worth 30, 40, and more times earnings." "Good growth stocks, like good wines, are often worth the price you have to pay" (p.113). Conversely, analysts were wrong about "tech stocks" in the 1990s, and many P/E ratios fell dramatically with the market correction of that time.

Conclusion

Recall that we stated in Chapter 2 that the amount a portfolio deviates from the market portfolio determines the risk of the portfolio. Investors may desire more or less risky portfolios than the market portfolio. The portfolio style and objectives reflect the investor's basic willingness to bear risk. While we recommend a balanced portfolio, some investors will want a more aggressive mix. Other investors may want a more conservative mix. Some investors only want "blue chip" stocks in their portfolios, while others desire portfolios built with small aggressive companies. Our approach works best if the investor uses the S & P 500 as the basic benchmark, chooses objectives and style for the portfolio, and then builds a portfolio based upon the sector and industry capitalization weightings of the S & P 500. While remaining close to the S & P 500 sector and industry weights, the investor can create varied portfolios of stocks across capitalization values and company management styles. Thus, while maintaining a diversified portfolio an investor can have a small cap, aggressive growth portfolio by focusing stock choices on those sectors emphasized by the strategist under the aggressive growth portfolio style and objective. The investor can check the portfolio against a style grid like that provided by Morningstar's Instant X-Ray. The performance of the portfolio can be checked against a benchmark portfolio for that style and objective.

How to Read the Advice of a Financial Strategist When Considering Style

When considering the advice of the financial strategist, understand that she will seldom recommend more than a 30 percent differential weighting from the market sector weights. Specifically, if a sector represents 20 percent of the market, it is unusual to see a strategist recommend more than a 26 percent or less than a 14 percent weighting in that sector. Some portfolios that are highly stylized are exceptions. The strategist places heavier weightings than normal because these portfolios represent only a portion of the market. Most investors own both growth and value portfolios. The blended allocations of their total investments come closer to the S & P 500 weightings. In most

---

cases, the only times a strategist goes beyond the 30 percent boundary is when the sector represents a very small part of the market, or if the portfolio objective is much different from that of the market. Some common examples of portfolios with different objectives than the market would be very conservative or aggressive growth portfolios. The conservative portfolio manager will generally have a much less volatile portfolio than an aggressive growth manager. The aggressive portfolio is accepting higher risk and more concentration, shooting for better returns, realizing that there may be a price to be paid in down markets.

CHAPTER 5

How Do We Begin?

The Use of the Investment Strategist and Market Sector Recommendations

In the next three chapters, we introduce types of investment research from three sources. This chapter formally introduces the research of the investment strategist, and suggests an approach to using it. Chapter 6 discusses technical analysis and its uses, and Chapter 7 introduces research of the industry analyst and discusses how to use it.

Large brokerage houses and investment managers employ investment strategists to forecast how trends in technological and economic growth will affect publicly-traded companies within market sectors and industries. Strategists are highly-educated individuals with advanced degrees in finance and economics. Senior strategists have years of experience and track records of results. Strategists start the process of making their portfolio recommendations by examining economic data including current market valuations. They analyze how various industries have behaved in the past in response to economic developments. Industries that have had similar responses are grouped together and identified as **sectors**. Strategists make recommendations to over-weight or under-weight different sectors and industries of the market based upon their analyses. These weightings suggest the most attractive sectors and industries in the market for investing and provide a method for managing risk and adding the often elusive alpha.

Market Sectors

Different investment strategists segment the economy in different ways. Strategists choose groups of industries that behave similarly in response to economic shocks and that have a logical connection. There are several variants of the basic set of market sectors depending upon the strategists' views about how best to organize a portfolio and diversify risk. The differences are slight, and there is no quantifiable reason to select one sector configuration over another. Exhibits 5-1 and 5-2 provide two groupings of market sectors from two strategists and include market capitalization weights for the stocks represented in each sector of the market.

Exhibit 5-1
S & P Market Sector/Master Grouping
and Market Capitalization Weights

Sector Group	Market Weight
Financials	17.7%
Services	4.9%
Consumer Staples	22.2%
Consumer Cyclicals	7.5%
Technology	22.2%
Capital Goods - Industrial	8.9%
Energy	7.2%
Basic Industry	2.6%
Transportation	0.5%
Utilities	6.3%

Exhibit 5-2
Alternative Market Sector Grouping
and Market Capitalization Weights

Sector Group	Market Weight
Consumer Discretionary	13%
Consumer Staples	8%
Energy	7%
Financials	18%
Health Care	14%
Industrials	11%
Information Technology	16%
Materials	3%
Telecommunications Services	6%
Utilities/MLPs/REITs	4%

Beyond the basic sector groupings for companies, strategists group companies into industries within each sector. Specifically, Exhibits 5-3 and 5-4 show two sectors, financials and consumer staples, and the associated industries within those sectors according to one source.[1] The exhibits also provide market capitalization weights for the sector and for the industries. Market capitalization weights change with the price of the stocks in the industries, so these numbers describe one distinct period in time.

Exhibit 5-3
Financial Sector and Industries
Market Sector Weight: 18%

Industry	Market Weight
Banks Major Regional	4.7%
Banks Money Center	1.7%
Consumer Finance	0.8%
Financial Diversified	4.3%
Insurance Brokers	0.4%
Insurance Life/Health	0.4%
Insurance Multi-line	0.8%
Insurance Property/Casualty	1.1%
Investment Banking/Brokerage	0.8%
Investment Management	0.1%
Savings & Loan Companies	0.5%

Exhibit 5-4
Consumer Staples Sector and Industries
Market Sector Weight: 12%

Industry	Market Weight
Beverages Alcoholic	0.4%
Beverages Non-Alcoholic	2.7%
Broadcasting (Television, Radio, Cable)	0.6%
Distributors Food & Health	0.8%
Entertainment	1.1%
Foods	1.5%
Household Products (Non-Durables)	1.8%
Housewares	0.3%
Personal Care	0.5%
Restaurants	0.6%
Retail (Drug Stores)	0.5%
Retail (Food Chains)	0.6%
Services (Employment)	0.0%
Specialty Printing	0.1%
Tobacco	1.2%

Market capitalization is the stock price multiplied by the number of shares outstanding each month. The market weight is the percentage a stock, industry or sector holds in the overall market capitalization. Stock prices rise and fall, thus market weights do the same. As you examine Exhibit 5-5, notice how sector weights changed between 1985 and 2001. The market may "move" a particular sector quite dramatically. The exposure that occurs from market dynamics should be effectively managed, and generally investors need advice about how to do so. The industry strategist is positioned to give such advice.

Exhibit 5-5

S & P 500 Historical Sector Weights: 1985–2001

Sector	1985	1987	1989	1991	1993	1995	1997	1998	1999	2000	2001
Basic Materials	8.3	9.3	8.4	7.4	7.7	6.6	4.4	.3	2.9	2.6	2.7
Capital Goods	10.1	10.3	10	9.3	9.5	9.3	9	7.9	8.4	9.1	9.1
Communication Svcs	8.3	8.2	10.4	8.3	9.5	8.8	6	7.9	8	6	6.6
Consumer Cyclicals	12.5	12.2	11.2	11.5	13.2	10	9.6	9.4	9.3	8.2	8.7
Consumer Staples	12.9	14.8	16.8	19.2	17.1	17.1	16.4	14.4	11.2	12.8	12.1
Energy	9	9.1	10.3	8.3	8.1	7.3	7.1	5.1	4.9	6.8	6.8
Financial	8.7	7.5	8	8.3	10.4	12.3	15.7	15.7	13	17	17.8
Health Care	6.8	7.6	8.9	12.8	8.5	10.8	11.7	12.4	9.3	13.5	14.8
Technology	13.5	12.1	7.5	6.9	7.8	11.3	15.1	20.6	30	19.5	17.1
Transportation	3.1	2.7	2	1.9	2.2	1.7	1.3	1	0.7	0.7	0.7
Utilities	7	6.2	6.5	6.2	6	4.7	3.8	3.2	2.3	4	3.9

How Do We Begin?

Let's look at Exhibit 5-5 for a few examples of market dynamics and the potential exposure from stock portfolio over time. In the early 1980s, the energy sector represented over 20 percent of the S & P 500 market value. As you can see from the exhibit, the value that sector represents in the market portfolio steadily decreased over time. Currently, the market valuation is around seven percent. It would have been an excellent investment strategy to under-weight the energy sector over the past 20 years. If an investor had holdings within the energy sector purchased in 1985, and simply sat on those holdings over the time period, slower than average growth in energy market prices would have reduced the weight of energy holdings in the portfolio. If these movements were anticipated, a savvy investor would have invested in more favorable sectors of the market and improved performance.

The financial sector, the technology sector and the health care sector all have shown very positive trends over the last 15 years. The growth in the portfolio weights reflects economic growth in the firms within those sectors. It is not hard to link what we know about an aging world population to growth in profitability in the health care sector, or the massive innovation in the management of information to growth in the technology sector. The growth in the financial sector reflects de-regulation and an environment of falling interest rates. Major trends reflect themselves in the sector weightings over time.

The technology sector is particularly interesting in its volatility over the time period. In 1985, technology comprised 13 percent of the market and declined consistently until 1992 when it made up seven percent of the S & P 500. After 1992, the technology sector literally drove the market growth of 1990s as the sector approached weights over 30 percent. When the "technology bubble" of the late 1990s finally burst, the sector declined dramatically in value, and by the year 2001 only comprised 20 percent of the S & P 500. Anticipating these trends is very important for risk management within a stock portfolio.

How do I Use Information About Market Sector and Sector Weights?

For a core portfolio style, a strategist seldom recommends over-weighting a sector by more than 20 percent, but many investors take much more risky positions without knowing it. For other more aggressive portfolio styles, strategists may make more aggressive weighting recommendations. Let's say that a strategist likes the technology sector, and that the sector currently comprises 20 percent of the market capitalization of the S & P 500 industries, thus it has a 20 percent weight in the market portfolio. If the strategist recommends allocating 24 percent of the portfolio to technology, it can be interpreted as a strong recommendation toward that sector. When individuals construct their portfolios, it is not unusual to observe portfolios constructed with 50 percent of their holdings in sectors that only comprise five percent of the market! Few investors understand the nature of the risk that they are assuming when they construct portfolios in this manner. They believe that their portfolios are diversified, because they have many stocks and mutual funds. A portfolio can have many assets, but still be terribly out of balance. Unless the portfolio is allocated across sectors in line with the market weights, it is not reaping the full benefits of diversification.

There are two different ways to use sector analysis when building or managing portfolios. The first approach is to keep the portfolio sectors and industries neutral to the market. This means that the market capitalization weights of your portfolio's holdings should mirror the weights of the benchmark. With this approach, the goal is to minimize the market sector and industry risk by mirroring the market capitalization weights of the baseline portfolio, and relying on stock choice to add value to the portfolio. Neutral portfolios vary with style emphasis, depending upon whether the emphasis is on value or growth, or on "small," "mid" or "large" cap stocks. The second approach is to use economic and strategist research to identify the best sectors and industries, and then to over and under-weight the sectors and industries, based upon the strategist's recommendations. Only after the weights for sectors and industries are chosen does the investor look more specifically at stocks.

By keeping your portfolio neutral with respect to the market weights, you minimize the risk of missing large "up" trends in a particular sector, but you also expose yourself to potential losses if the market suddenly moves a sector in the negative direction. You are only protected from trends like the technology bubble and its bursting by wisely choosing stocks that are either less volatile than the sector overall, or are immune to the bursting of the bubble. This approach uses the information of the industry strategist to focus research efforts on the stocks in the sectors and industries expected to grow more quickly than the market, and minimizes research efforts on the stocks in those industries expected to grow more slowly than the market. The other approach is to use the strategist's weighting advice. With this approach, the investor is more exposed to the risks associated with bad forecasts, but there is the potential for great gains if the forecasts are correct.

An investor may desire a more risky portfolio, but it is highly recommend that he understand how to construct a portfolio in line with the market. There are a couple of ways to take a more aggressive position in a portfolio if desired. One is to make large bets by heavily over-weighting favored sectors or industries. The second is to buy small, more aggressive companies across all sectors and industries. The second approach provides a more diversified portfolio, avoiding concentration risk, but may expose you to more company-specific risk. We will discuss more about enhancing portfolio performance in Chapters 10 and 11.

How Does a Strategist Predict Trends?

Strategists specialize in forecasting major economic trends, based upon demographic changes, technological developments, and shortages of raw materials. They use a combination of formal statistical modeling and good common sense. Strategists predict changing market sentiments. A good strategist is a bit of a psychologist. He understands how conflict can lead to the stockpiling of certain goods, simply because people need to stockpile to feel secure. He understands how optimism increases spending on consumer goods, and more importantly, he understands the factors that affect consumers' moods.

How Do We Begin?

Some strategists specialize in observing the behavior of policy makers, like Alan Greenspan at the Federal Reserve. Others follow politics and use trends in legislation and national political mood to predict economic growth. In general, strategists make recommendations based upon whether they think there are underlying factors that will affect the overall profitability of stocks within a given sector.

Why Does a Strategist Recommend a Sector be Over (Under) –Weighted?

Strategists will over (under) -weight an economic sector because they believe the sector will out (under) -perform the other sectors in the market in the near future. (Strategists are often "early" in their forecasts. They see a trend before the rest of the market sees it.) They come to their conclusions regarding relative market performance based upon their forecasts of major economic and psychological trends that affect the profitability of firms within the various sectors of the market.

For example, a falling interest rate-environment tends to be highly profitable for financial institutions. Over the 16-year period between 1985-2001, interest rates steadily declined as the threat of world inflation declined. Unexpected inflation is deadly for financial institutions, because it eliminates the profits from loaning money. If a bank loans $1,000 at 10 percent for one year, it received $1,100 at the end of the year. If inflation is zero, then the profit from the loan is the $100 minus any costs associated with making the loan. On the other hand, if inflation suddenly rises to 10 percent, the bank earns $1,100, but it is only worth $1,000 in purchasing power. Inflation erodes the value of the currency. Banks care about purchasing power, or the real return. The real return is defined as the nominal return (10 percent) minus the inflation rate (10 percent). In this case, the real return equals zero percent. The lender loses and the borrower receives a free loan. On the other hand, unexpected disinflation provides a windfall to lenders. Thus, financial institutions tend to do well in an environment of falling interest rates. A good strategist would identify the falling interest rate trend and recommend that investors over-weight the financial sector of the economy.

What are the Pros and Cons of Using Sector Analysis?

First, while sector analysis is a very valuable tool, you should remember that it is simply that, a tool. Remember that humans make forecasts. No one can perfectly predict the future. The most educated and informed strategist can still be terribly wrong. No one could have predicted the terrible events of September 11, 2001 that had a profound effect on the markets. No one can predict droughts or floods that have major implications for profitability. Human behavior is highly unpredictable. People are fickle. There may be current trends in the market that the best strategist might underestimate. It is important to examine other sources of information beyond strategists' reports.

Second, there are times when the sector groups are dominated by the performance of one company, and failing to understand this leads to major mistakes in portfolio construction. For example, Exhibit 5-6 shows that in a sector grouping of the past, the capital goods sector was dominated by the electrical equipment industry, and General Electric (G.E.). If you look closely, you'll see that G.E. stock comprised almost four percent of the entire S & P 500 index. G.E. also comprised 80 percent of the electrical equipment industry, almost half of the entire capital goods sector. With this sector grouping, a strategists who recommends over (under) -weighting the capital goods sector is really saying he thinks G.E. will do well (or poorly). What makes this problematic is that over the last 10 years, much of the growth of G.E. (roughly half its income) came from financial services. Strategists alter groupings to adjust for these types of problems, but as the G.E. example shows, sometimes problems like this occur for extended periods of time.

Exhibit 5-6
Capital Goods Sector
Focus on Electrical Equipment Companies
Market Weight: 9.1%

Industry	Market Weight
Aerospace/Defense	0.83%
Containers Metal and Glass	0.02%
Electrical Equipment	4.74%
American Power Conversion	0.02%
Cooper Industries	0.04%
Emerson Electric	0.22%
General Electric	**3.97%**
Honeywell International Inc.	0.23%
Molex Inc.	0.0435%
Jabil Circuit Inc.	0.04%
Rockwell International Corp.	0.03%

Industry	Market Weight
Sanmia Corp.	0.05%
Solectron Corp.	0.08%
Symbol Technologies Inc.	0.03%
Thomas & Betts Corp.	0.01%
Engineering and Construction	0.04%
Machinery Diversified	0.39%
Manufacturing Diversified	2.51%
Manufacturing Special	0.14%
Office Equipment and Supplies	0.1%
Trucks and Parts	0.07%
Waste Management	0.21%

In this case, G.E.'s large weight in the capital goods sector makes following the strategist's advice tricky. If you over-weight capital goods but choose to purchase Honeywell stock, you could be making an enormous mistake! Investing in other electrical companies may or may not be a good idea. You need more information. This is where an excellent broker or securities analyst factors into the analysis.[2]

In January 2002, Standard and Poor's addressed the issue of industry and sector weighting imbalances and other issues related to market developments by reclassifying sector and industry groups. Their old standards and new standards are available on their Web site, and they provide historical data for the new classifications. There are limited problems now with "industries of one," where an industry group is comprised of one company, a problem that was quite prevalent in the past. S & P re-classified G.E. as well, but over time the type of problem identified in Exhibit 5-6 could evolve again.

How Do We Begin?

Market dynamics affect indices. There is no getting around this fact.

The Industry Level

Once you identify the sectors that look the most attractive at a given time, identify the industries within that sector that are expected to outperform the market. Exhibit 5-7 provides a list of sectors with their associated industries, published regularly by one investment firm. The exhibit also includes the market weight held by each sector/industry, and a recommendation from the strategist about where to over-weight. Notice that with the core portfolio, the recommended weights are significantly different from the actual weights, but they are not so different as to cause excess risk to a portfolio.

A "+" sign indicates that the strategist likes that industry. Notice that the strategist lists recommended weights for the portfolio in terms of sectors. If you were to take the strategist's advice, based upon data from October 2001 in Exhibit 5-7, you would over-weight the following sectors: communications services, consumer staples, financial, technology and utilities (only slightly). You should focus your search on the industries within those sectors that have a "+" recommendation.

Using this information does two things to help investors and financial advisors. The first benefit comes from the fact that trends continue for fairly long periods of time. Strategists make changes in their recommendations slowly. Therefore, by just reviewing the recommendations of your chosen strategist once a month, you gain a global view of his total market recommendations and can easily observe what has changed from the last month. Most months nothing will have changed. When there is a change of measurable weighting, particularly a change from over to under-weighting and vice versa, you have a focus for your research efforts. When changes do happen, strategists tend to catch them before the market catches them. You have time to do the research.

The second benefit gained is that if you spend an hour a month reviewing this information, you will stay well informed about major trends and shifts in those trends. Research is more focused and takes less time than if you tried to read stacks of magazines and news-papers or do on-line research.

Another time saver limits the number of industries to research by avoiding sectors that represent a tiny part of the overall S & P. For example, you might avoid sectors like basic industries or transportation, based upon the October 2001 weights. You might also avoid heavily-weighting stocks in industries with tiny market weights. Your search is quickly narrowed in this manner. Continue narrowing your search by focusing your search toward the favored industries. There is no point in doing research on every industry within a sector, when it is likely that those industries out-of-favor will under-perform the S & P 500. It is better to own the average stock in the best market sector/industry, than the best stock in the poorest-performing market sector.

Exhibit 5-7
Sector: Basic Material

Market Weight: 3.0%   **Recommended Weight: 2.7%**

Industry	Market Weight	
Agricultural Products	0.09%	
Aluminum	0.39%	
Chemicals	1.01%	"+"
Chemicals: Diversified	0.14%	"+"
Chemicals: Specialty	0.24%	"+"
Construction Cement & Aggregates	0.05%	
Containers & Packaging	0.07%	
Gold & Metals Mining	0.19%	
Iron & Steel	0.07%	
Metals Mining	0.06%	
Paper & Forest Products	0.51%	

Sector: Capital Goods

Market Weight: 9.01%   **Recommended Weight: 8%**

Industry	Market Weight	
Aerospace/Defense	0.83%	
Containers Metal and Glass	0.17%	
Electrical Equipment	4.74%	"+"
Engineering and Construction	0.04%	"+"
Machinery Diversified	0.39%	"+"
Manufacturing Diversified	2.51%	
Manufacturing Special	0.14%	
Office Equipment and Supplies	0.1%	
Trucks and Parts	0.07%	
Waste Management	0.21%	

Sector: Communication Service

Market Weight: 6.62%   **Recommended Weight: 8%**

Industry	Market Weight	
Cellular/Wireless	0.46%	"+"
Telecommunications: Long Distance	1.76%	"+"
Telephone	4.4%	"+"

Sector: Consumer Cyclicals

Market Weight: 8.67%   **Recommended Weight: 7%**

Industry	Market Weight	
Automobiles	0.58%	
Auto Parts & Equipment	0.27%	
Building Materials	0.1%	
Consumer: Jewelry, Novelties & Gifts	0.08%	
Footwear	0.1%	
Gaming/Lottery	0.03%	
Hardware & Tools	0.06%	
Homebuilding	0.6%	
Household Furnishing & Appliances	0.1%	
Leisure Time: Products	0.25%	
Lodging/Hotel/Gaming	0.26%	
Publishing: Newspaper	0.41%	
Retail: Building Supplies	1.26%	
Retail: Computer & Electronics	0.18%	"+"
Retail: Department Stores	0.42%	
Retail: Discounters	0.15%	
Retail: General Merchandise	3.01%	"+"
Retail: Specialty	0.29%	"+"
Retail: Specialty Apparel	0.29%	"+"
Services: Commercial & Consumer	0.31%	
Textiles	0.06%	

Sector: Consumer Staples

Market Weight: 10.08%   Recommended Weight: 12%

Industry	Market Weight	
Beverages Alcoholic	0.44%	
Beverages Non-Alcoholic	2.37%	"+"
Broadcasting (Television, Radio, Cable)	0.61%	
Distributors Food & Health	0.76%	
Entertainment	1.06%	
Foods	1.47%	
Household Products (Non-Durables)	1.80%	
Housewares	0.13%	
Personal Care	0.47%	"+"
Restaurants	0.63%	
Retail (Drug Stores)	0.52%	"+"
Retail (Food Chains)	0.56%	"+"
Specialty Printing	0.06%	
Tobacco	1.19%	

Sector: Energy

Market Weight: 6.84%   Recommended Weight: 5%

Industry	Market Weight	
Oil & Gas: Drilling & Exploration	0.66%	"+"
Oil & Gas: Exploration & Production	0.51%	
Oil & Gas: Refining & Marketing	0.06%	
Oils: Domestic Integrated	0.58%	
Oils: International Integrated	5.03%	"+"

Sector: Financials

Market Weight: 17.85%   Recommended Weight: 20%

Industry	Market Weight	
Banks Major Regional	4.65%	"+"
Banks Money Center	1.70%	"+"
Consumer Finance	0.82%	"+"
Financial Diversified	4.30%	"+"
Insurance Brokers	0.40%	"+"
Insurance Life/Health	0.83%	"+"
Insurance Multi-line	2.58%	"+"
Insurance Property/Casualty	1.05%	
Investment Banking/Brokerage	0.82%	
Investment Management	0.14%	"+"
Savings & Loan Companies	0.52%	

Sector: Health Care

Market Weight: 14.79%   Recommended Weight: 11%

Industry	Market Weight	
Biotechnology	0.75%	"+"
Diversified	4.86%	"+"
Hospital Management	0.44%	"+"
Drug/Major Pharmaceuticals	6.72%	"+"
Generic Drugs	0.06%	"+"
HMOs	0.37%	
Long Term and Managed Care	0.03%	
Medical Products & Supplies	1.47%	"+"
Specialized Services	0.09%	

Sector: Technology

Market Weight: 17.10% Recommended Weight: 21%

Industry	Market Weight	
Communication Equipment	1.44%	
Computer Hardware	3.12%	"+"
Computer Networking	1.01%	"+"
Computer Software & Services	5.97%	"+"
Computer Peripherals	0.34%	
Electronics: Component Distributors	0.04%	
Electronics: Defense	0.13%	
Electronics: Instrumentation	0.10%	
Electronics: Semiconductors	2.70%	"+"
Equipment: Semiconductors	0.59%	"+"
Photography/Imaging	0.61%	
Servicing Computer Systems	0.64%	
Servicing Data Processing	0.85%	"+"

Sector: Transportation

Market Weight: 0.69%   Recommended Weight: 0%

Industry	Market Weight	
Airlines	0.19%	
Railroads	0.38%	
Truckers	0.01%	
Air Freight	0.12%	"+"

Sector: Utilities

Market Weight: 3.58%   **Recommended Weight: 4%**

Industry	Market Weight	
Electric Utilities	2.56%	
Natural Gas	0.95%	
Power Producers (Independent)	0.07%	"+"

Caveats for the Individual Investor

Individual investors should use recommended sector/industry weights with care. Most individual investors have portfolios of between 10 and 30 stocks. On the other hand, a core institutional portfolio will have between 75 and 200 individual stocks. There are many specialty or focused institutional portfolios and mutual funds that are much more concentrated, but these portfolios normally represent a small part of a larger portfolio. An individual investor with an average of 20 stocks generally will not hold stocks in all of the recommended industries. The individual portfolio is likely to be more concentrated than the institutional portfolio, but the individual can still reap the benefits of good diversification.

Conclusion

If an investor takes a long-run view of the stock market, he understands that the market is cyclical and that there is a positive upward trend over time. Over the long run, cyclical moves in the market, trends in different sectors and industries, and different investment

100

styles tend to balance out. Even the best investment strategist cannot perfectly predict catastrophes and technological innovations that change industries dramatically, or investment strategies that capture the public's imagination. Portfolio construction addresses the fact that there is risk associated with holding financial assets, and allows investors to make deliberate decisions based on how they see the market and their own tolerance for risk.

Most investors' portfolios are dramatically out-of-balance with the market. Being significantly out-of- balance with the market creates excess risk. The investor is placing big bets, often without knowing it. While we are advocating that investors over-weight the best sectors/industries in their portfolio to earn alpha, we are not advocating the creation of portfolios that are so dramatically different from the market that they create huge exposures to risk.

It might seem easy to identify major market trends, but most individuals are not very good at it. Trust people who devote their careers to this task to do this for you. The strategist is the starting point. For all but the most experienced investor, creating a balanced portfolio is not a "do-it-yourself" project. Most of the best comprehensive and consistent information is available through major brokerage firms. They provide accessible and organized information based upon excellent research practices. They have a comparative advantage in this area. Only seldom does a major research strategist take an extreme position that would lead to too risky a portfolio. Strategists remain consistent from period to period, so their recommendations are easy to review in a few minutes each month. Most changes they make will be minor. If a strategist does make a major change in his recommendations, this provides a significant flag to an investor that it is time to do thoughtful and deliberate research into the new recommendations.

Because strategists have specialized areas of interest and expertise, and because forecasts are imperfect, we recommend using a secondary source for strategists' recommendations. Compare your secondary source with your primary source to identify discrepancies. If there are significant discrepancies, check the two views against relative strength and analyst reports (see Chapters 6 and 7). Find consistency across research sources. One strategist may be early in his forecasts about changing trends or there may be real differences in their opinions. During times of market turbulence and uncertainty, you may see significantly different views across strategists. If you cannot find consistency, you are probably better off hugging the index for a while. Avoid making large bets on sectors where research is inconsistent.

CHAPTER 6

The Use of Technical Analysis

How to Use Absolute and Relative Strength
Analysis to Confirm Strategists' Opinions

*"It is not a case of choosing those which, to the
best of one's judgment, are really the prettiest, nor even
those which average opinion genuinely thinks the prettiest...we devote our intelligences to anticipating what
average opinion expects the average opinion to be."*
John Maynard Keynes, <u>The General Theory of
Employment, Interest, and Money</u>, 1936, op. cit. p. 155.

This chapter introduces a second type of research
useful in constructing a balanced portfolio — a
simple technical model that allows the investor
to see how a sector or industry is doing relative to the
market. As the quote above indicates, predicting what
the market will favor is very important in portfolio con-

struction and stock selection. This type of research provides a second opinion to the strategist's recommendations, and is the second step in the process of using securities research.

Market Timing: What Not to do!

Market timing means moving assets in or out of the equity markets in an attempt to increase returns. The motivation behind this approach is to be in the market during upswings and out of the market during downswings. Knowing where the market is going has long been an obsession of investors. In fact, many investors stay less than fully invested in the market because they simply cannot believe that the market will go any higher. One of the most frequently asked questions for investing is "What is the market going to do?" It is a huge mistake to try to answer this question if the goal is to make significant "pin point" decisions on putting money in the market or selling stocks to take money out of the market with the intent of reinvesting later when the market is down. Timing the market is not something managers, brokers or clients do very well. Market timing is difficult. Exhibit 6-1 illustrates the basic problem. The exhibit shows the S & P 500 levels from 1987 to 2001, over the period of the bull market and the subsequent correction. Notice the large upward movements that follow downturns.

Exhibit 6-1
Staircase Bull Market

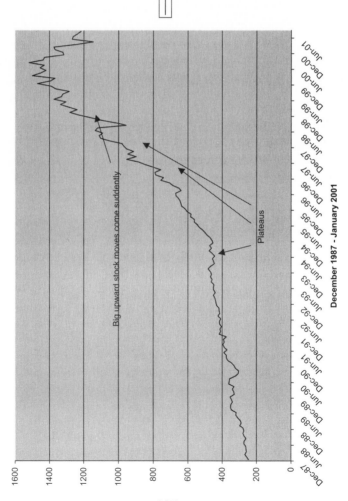

105

Investment Survival

Markets spend long periods in plateaus and then move in very strong spurts. When the markets move, they move strongly and swiftly, both up and down. Because the long-term trend of the markets is up, to participate in the "up side" of the market, money has to be in the market when it moves up. If an investor is less than fully invested in the stock market during a large upswing, the opportunity is lost and can never be recaptured. On the other hand, when markets move down sharply, they recover. For example, in 1981, the market lost 24.13 percent of its value, but took only 83 days to reach new highs. A similar pattern is seen when examining the 1987 crash. The market lost 36.13 percent of its value on October 19, 1987, but had reached new highs in less than two years. In fact, for the full year of 1987, the Dow was positive three percent!

Exhibit 6-2 shows just how dramatic markets can be. There were about 2,300 trading days from 1980 to 1989. By missing just 10 of the best days in the market, five percent of the entire decade's performance was lost. As more good days are eliminated, one can see that by missing just 1.7 percent of the best trading days, a majority of the performance was lost. This pattern of dramatic upswings and downturns continued through the 1990s and is present today. We don't want to suggest that any investor would have such bad luck as to be out of the market on just those specific days, yet the point is clear — failing to be fully invested when the market rallies strongly means losing opportunities that may never be recaptured.

Exhibit 6-2
The Risk of Missing the Best Days
in the Market

	1980s	1990s
Fully-Invested Earnings	27.86%	17.5%
Minus 10 Best	19.12%	12.6%
Minus 20 Best	13.6%	9.3%
Minus 30 Best	9%	6.5%
Minus 40 Best	4.94%	3.9%

Therefore, avoid market timing. It is more dangerous to be out of the market when it is rising than to be fully invested during the bad times. While the market crash of 1987 was very scary, those who stayed in the market through the price decline were well positioned for the strong market that followed, provided they rebalanced their portfolios. Many of the investors who sold prior to the decline failed to reinvest, and were not well positioned for the next several years of strong markets that followed.

We are not advocating a passive investment plan. There is significant evidence that actively-managed portfolios out-perform passively-managed ones, and that stock picking matters, but we are firmly saying that for the average investor, a long-term approach of choosing stocks for a balanced portfolio is better.[1] An actively-managed portfolio should be oriented toward the longer term, but have a short to medium-term goal of out-performing the S & P 500 index. There are asset allocation strategies that are meaningful for shifting money into or out of the equity market to support a predetermined risk management asset allocation policy. We also highly recommend purchasing more stock when the market is low, and less when it is high. This method is called "dollar cost averaging" and is discussed in Chapter 10. Dollar cost averaging is one of the oldest investment concepts, and it works.

Using Market Trends and Technical Models in Portfolio Construction

Researchers have written volumes on the use of technical analysis. One of the most popular books on the subject is by Robert Edwards and John Magee. Technical Analysis of Stock Trends was first published in 1948, and has just been revised in its eighth edition. Most industry insiders see this book as the "bible" of technical analysis since it is an exhaustive treatise on all aspects of this type of analysis, with the possible exception of "point and figure charting." It is also written for the layperson and not the Wall Street expert.

Technical analysis differs from its cousin, fundamental analysis, because it only deals with price and volume information, rather than more "fundamental variables" like earnings per share, dividend ratios and news on macroeconomic trends. The theory supporting technical analysis says that all relevant information about a company, such as earnings, growth rates, new product development and taxes are evaluated by the marketplace, and the sum total of what everyone thinks about all of these things is displayed in the price and volume action of the company's securities.

The Use of Technical Analysis

If the information about a company is not perfect, that is to say if everyone in the market does not have access to it at the same time, but rather they gain access to information slowly over time, price and volume action will give hints of future trends in stock prices. Therefore, by studying price and volume information, one can use the data to predict future stock prices.

More intuitively, technical analysis involves the supply and demand for a security. If there are more buyers than sellers of a stock, the stock price rises. If there are more sellers of a stock than buyers, the stock price falls. Volume has an augmenting or diminishing effect. It is considered more bullish if stocks are rising in price on heavy volume (a larger volume that is normal for the stock), and less bullish if the price rises on lower than normal volume. On the sell side, heavy volume on declining prices predicts more bearish behavior, and a declining stock price on lower than normal volume indicates a less bearish future view. Market psychology is important because price movements result from the total number of trades in the market, and participants try to anticipate the general mood of the market when placing their buy and sell orders.

One ongoing debate about the viability of technical analysis is between those who believe that expectations are rational, making stock prices random, and therefore unpredictable, and those who believe that market psychology is not completely rational. If the market is completely efficient and stock prices are random, only new information — information that is unavailable to anyone prior to its becoming public — will affect stock prices. On the other hand, if markets are less than perfectly efficient — there is inside information, inadequate or asymmetric information — then there may be patterns in stock behavior that will persist and can be used to predict future stock prices.

Some argue that if a researcher were to come across a technical model that predicted stock prices well, he would keep it a guarded secret, and use it to earn excess returns in the markets. He certainly wouldn't write a book about the model and share it with the world, because if the technical model became well known, it would quickly lose its usefulness to the researcher. His excess returns would be wiped out by market trading around the information generated by his model. It is important to keep this criticism of technical models in mind when you come across anyone who tells you that he has discovered a model of the stock market that works and will make you rich.

In spite of the debate around technical modeling, there are literally hundreds of technical indicators used to predict stock prices. Some of them appear very logical, while others stretch the imagination. Some relatively sophisticated smoothing functions, oscillators and mathematical techniques are combined with charts of "pennants and flags and double bottoms." For the non-professional, most of these techniques are either too complicated or too strange to even consider as part of an investment strategy.

One of the technical indicators that we do find useful and that we recommend investors use when construct-ing a portfolio is "relative strength" analysis. There are trends in market sectors and industries that remain posi-tive or negative for periods longer than a day or month.

Sometimes trends run across years. Relative strength analysis can be used to identify market perceptions about those trends and is fairly simple to understand. Relative strength should not be used on its own, but as a check on other sources of information.

Perceptions are often more important than truth when it comes to trading stocks. The key over the short to medium run is to identify market perceptions, even if they differ from the truth. What good is it if you hold information about a company that is positive if other investors can't access that information until a date in the very distant future? If you purchase the stock, others will *not* follow suit and you have a stock that isn't seeing much market action. If you knew with certainty the information about the company would become public at a particular date, you would want to hold other more profitable stocks until the day prior to the information becoming public. Then you would want to purchase the stock and yield the large return on the information. If you held the stock the entire long time period, you would have missed the opportunity to hold stocks that were yielding higher returns in the short to medium term. The point is that what others know and do affect the returns of your portfolio. A way to get a picture of what others are thinking is with relative strength models. They provide information on market sentiments.

Relative strength analysis provides an opinion about a sector or industry group. You are able to assess price trends relative to the market as a whole, and compare individual industries' price performance to that of others. Use relative strength to check the opinions of the market strategist.

How to Use the Charts

The charts we discuss here have two parts. The first chart is of the absolute price movements of a sector or industry. The second chart is of the same price movements, but is calculated by creating a ratio of the industry or sector price changes to the market, as defined by the S & P 500 Index. This type of information will enable you to see how a sector or industry is performing relative to the market, regardless of how the market is doing.

Trends in relative strength tend to last for many years. While the market has a lot of ups and downs — either sectors or industries are in-favor/out-performing the market, or out of favor/under-performing the market — these trends are much more consistent than the absolute price chart trends. A sector or industry that is underperforming the market in both up and down markets is quite obviously not an attractive part of the market.

When you look at a relative strength graph, you will see two lines, one for the relative strength measure plotted over time, and the other for that measure's 75-week moving average. There are some technical analysts who believe that there is some significance to a relative strength trend crossing its moving average line in either the positive or negative direction. We do not recommend using the charts in this manner. As you can see from the charts in this chapter, trends tend to persist, regardless of the overall market volatility. It is highly unusual to see a change in less that 18 months, and not unusual to see the relative strength of a sector or industry last for 10 to 15 years. **Environmental services** is an excellent example of a long trend in relative strength.

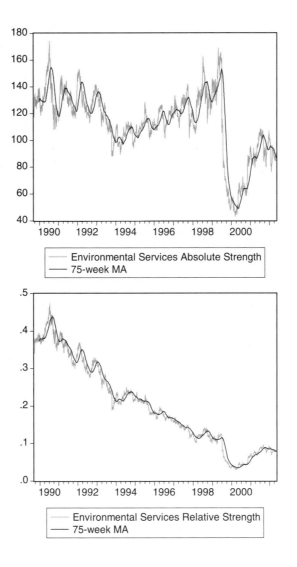

Environmental Services Absolute Strength
75-week MA

Environmental Services Relative Strength
75-week MA

Examples:

To help you to understand how relative strength charts are used, we have provided several examples. First, look at the S & P 500 absolute strength chart. This chart shows the market movements from September 1989 to May 2002. This chart will be useful for comparison, since it is the denominator of the relative strength number over time.

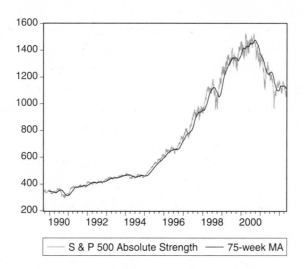

The charts of environmental services and the charts that follow will contain the following four elements: In the top panel you will see:

1. A line chart of the weekly close of the S & P's Industry Group Index since 1989, with the index range indicated to the left.

2. A line of the 75-week moving average of the S & P's Industry Group Index (this is the smoother line).

In the bottom panel you will see:

3. A relative strength line of the Standard & Poor's Industry group compared with the Standard & Poor's 500 Stock Index.

4. A line of the 75-week moving average of the relative strength measure.[2]

Not all sectors or industries are quite as clear examples as the following, but these examples should show how a combination of absolute and relative strength charts provide valuable information when analyzing portfolios.

Because relative strength is a ratio, when the market appreciates by 10 percent and the energy sector appreciates by 15 percent, the relative strength for the energy sector will rise. If the market depreciates by 10 percent and the energy sector depreciates by five percent, the energy sector will rise. The relative strength for a sector or industry will fall if the sector or industry index grows more slowly than the market or depreciates more than the market.

When using relative strength information, major shifts in trends will not immediately be obvious. Major moves take two to three months and longer before it is obvious that they have occurred. Thus a caveat about the use of these charts is to use them only for long-term investing, and only as a check on other sources. If you want to use technical models for short-term trading, you must find a different model than relative strength. Relative strength simply won't work for you. As an example, the technology sector chart on the next page shows a major trend reversal in 1999, but it took three to four months before it was fairly obvious from the chart that the change was beginning. It was only after a year of so that a major reversal was completely obvious.

The **technology sector** charts illustrate where the absolute strength and relative strength mirror each other. The technology sector out-performed the market between 1990 and 1999. Since 1999, these same technology stocks under-performed. This major trend reversal probably indicates the poor price trend relative to the market will persist.

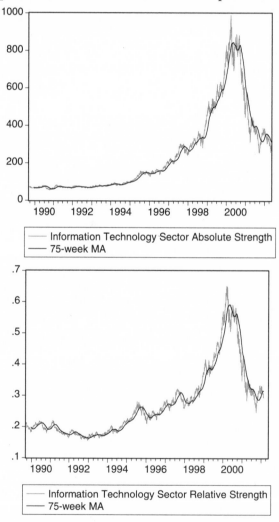

The **energy sector** charts provide a different picture. From 1990 until 2000, energy stocks were rising with the market, but the energy sector under-performed. The sector is improving relative to the market since 2000. The relative strength supports a strategist over-weighting this sector. Individual industries may differ.

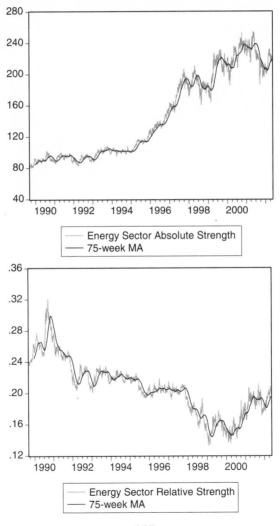

Starting in 2000, **specialty stores** also shows a change trend. It appears that both charts are making a smooth rounded change from down to up, a sign that retail specialty could be a very interesting industry to consider, if the strategist recommends this industry.

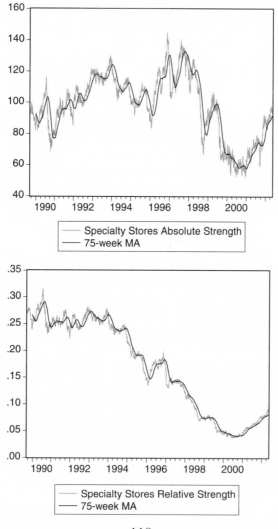

The **insurance health/life** industry shows the absolute price pumping up and down from 1997 forward. The relative strength in this industry suggests one might consider this industry, again only if the strategist recommends it.

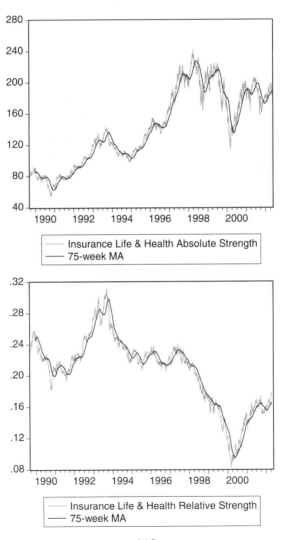

119

When Relative Strength Works — and When it Doesn't

Relative strength charts do not provide enough information to make specific investment decisions without fundamental research. The information is most useful when used in the following manner.

1. When using a strategist's research recommendations, investors are likely to identify more industries than they have funds with which to invest. For the individual investor, applying all of the strategist's recommendations would result in too many individual stocks given the size of the account. Therefore, relative strength is helpful in identifying those sectors and industries that both the strategist recommends, and where the current relative strength shows that the market also likes this market area.

2. Having identified several industries within a market sector, relative strength is very helpful in deciding which industry deserves more extensive research. It is not unusual that when additional fundamental research is reviewed, the industry does not look as attractive as the strategist or relative strength suggested. If that is the case, then the investor should move on to the next industry that has been recommended by both the strategist and relative strength data.

3. Relative strength is very helpful in raising the right questions to identify significant changes in the market. After a sector or industry shows a long trend of positive relative strength, a major downward trend should force the investor to take a very hard look at the stocks in the industries.

Re-examine the strategist's and industry analyst's information after a change in trend. The market will often show poor performance before either strategist or industry analyst give up on groups they have been favoring for some time.

4. Because select sectors and industries out-perform the market for long periods of time, when industries that have been in downward trends for a long period of time begin to show positive strength, it should alert investors to do more research on stocks in those industries.

5. When market trends turn on stocks that were previously out of favor, more information is published about them. In a normal screening process, an investor may not take these reports seriously because they are not companies or industries with which they are familiar. Unless the investor has long term experience in investing, it is not unusual that he has never seen a positive report on companies that have been out of favor for long periods. Watching relative strength is helpful in pointing out these changes to investors. They may pay more attention to fundamental research reports on industries coming newly into favor.

Because relative strength changes very slowly, it will take several months to establish a change of trend for an industry. Therefore it will only take 15 to 30 minutes a month to check these charts to see if anything has changed from the previous month. This is a very short investment of time to review the entire market to see if there are meaningful shifts. It is helpful to know that strong trends are continuing and no changes are indicated. When shifts are apparent, it is an excellent signal to see if similar or opposite shifts are happening in other industries. Evident shifts signal to the investor that he should begin looking at the fundamental research to gain a deeper understanding regarding the shifts.

Conclusion

Relative strength gives you a sense of market sentiment; it explains whether an industry is "in favor" or "out of favor." Measures of industry relative strength are available for approximately 110 sector and industry groups. Many full-service brokers have sources for industry relative strength data, but they are not used much. When investors do use technical data, they often misuse them by focusing upon the wrong types of information, or by looking at data that are geared toward the short-term trader. Technical data on Web sites are typically short-term oriented.

Technical analysis is based upon the idea that trends persist — that groups showing above-average performance will continue to do so, and that groups showing below-average performance will continue to under-perform the market. The greater the strength in relation to all other groups, the better the performance will be; and the longer a group maintains its performance trend, the more difficult it will be to reverse. On the other hand, if the relative strength is poor, the group's performance will be worse; and the longer the performance persists, the more significant the reversal will be.

Relative strength technical analysis should not be

used alone to select industries and sectors for consideration. It should provide additional information to the investor to better understand what the market is doing regardless of what the fundamental economic and earnings trends may be.

Once the sectors and industries of interest are identified (based upon the strategist's opinions), check the industries and sectors against relative strength. If you do so, you'll have a better idea of why you want to consider one industry over another. Relative strength often identifies industries that have been poor performers, but whose time has come and should now be considered for further analysis. Based upon the strategist's recommendations on sector and industry strength, and filtered through relative strength trends, you can identify a very focused group of industries to further research. Be careful though — relative strength is a tool, not an answer!

CHAPTER 7

The Use of the Analyst:
The Third Opinion

The Perils and Pitfalls of Analysts' Reports:
How to Interpret Their Recommendations

This chapter explains how to use the research provided by the industry analyst. This research is the third source of information that we recommend you use when constructing a stock portfolio. Major brokerage houses and many regional firms employ analysts, and provide high-quality research about industry groups. After you use the strategist's recommendations on market sectors and individual industries, and check those recommendations against relative strength trends, use analyst reports for a third opinion.

Industry analysts have unique knowledge. They are often Certified Financial Analysts (CFA) and are very knowledgeable about the industries they analyze. Analysts understand the pertinent financial reports provided by companies they cover, they know the management, the competitors and have broader contextual knowledge about markets and economic activity affecting their industries.

Industry analysts make recommendations about the specific companies in their industries. The first way that an investor should use analyst's reports is to look at the over-all opinion that the analyst has of his industry. This is a good indicator of whether the industry is a good candidate for investment.

Be Careful When Reading an Analyst's Stock Recommendations

One of the greatest problems with using individual stock research is failing to put it into perspective. In order to really understand what an analyst is saying, know who the analyst's primary audience is. The primary audience for securities analysts is the institutional investor and portfolio manager. Understanding the analyst's audience puts their opinions in perspective. The audience shapes the manner in which the analyst formulates opinions.

Because of the size of institutional portfolios, it is not unusual for an institution to buy a small amount of a stock in an industry that it has severely under-weighted. Institutions tend to hold portfolios of stocks that mirror the overall market much more closely than those of the average investor. Institutional portfolios are so large that they may purchase several thousand shares, representing only 10 percent of a normal weighting in a specific industry within the overall portfolio. Institutions want to know the best stock in a poorly-performing industry simply to keep track of what is happening within that industry. Institutions look to the market analysts for this information.

Because of the analyst's audience, analysts feel they must make "buy" recommendations on stocks in industries that they are not really excited about. Exhibit 7-1 provides an example of an analyst's recommendations on stocks within the specialty insurance industry. Notice that the analyst is neutral on the majority of stocks, and has one buy recommendation with XL Capital. If a broker simply examines this information out of context, he might recommend the purchase shares of XL Capital shares to his clients in spite of the analyst's neutral view on most of the firms within the industry. In this case, the analyst does not like this industry and is highlighting one company for reasons that have no value to the normal investor.

Exhibit 7-1
Insurance/Specialty

Company	Recommendation
Freemont General	Neutral
Frontier Insurance	Neutral
Meadowbrook Insurance	Neutral
Mercury General	Neutral
Progressive Corp.	Neutral
RLI Corp.	Neutral
XL Capital	Buy
Swiss Re.	Neutral

1 Buy and 7 Neutral
Source: Goldman Sachs Americas Research: June 2000

Each analyst is entitled to have one buy recommendation within an industry in order to "keep face" in front of buy-side analysts and portfolio managers, even if he is not positive on the entire industry. Buy recommendations can be disastrous for the individual investor. We are not suggesting that the one buy recommendation is a bad investment, we are only pointing out that by looking at the entire list of stocks and the recommendations on those stocks, we have additional information that we can use. If an analyst has an overall gloomy view of his industry, we may want to research stocks in industries where the analyst has a more positive outlook. There are a number of stories on Wall Street where an analyst singles out one great stock in a lousy industry. On the other hand, there are many stories about poker players drawing to an inside straight. The reason the stories are told and re-told is because they represent rare events. The investor who follows the analyst's advice may win big, but this is the exception, not the rule. Investors are better off by playing a higher-probability game.

How do I use the Information of the Analyst to Make Industry Choices?

Look at all of the opinions of a stock analyst within an industry to see how many companies he really likes within that industry. If the analyst has mostly negative opinions of the stocks in their group, and you see only one BUY recommendation, *beware*. Purchasing that stock for an individual investor could become a huge mistake. Put the stock decision into an overall context. There are several rules of thumb to follow:

- If your analyst provides a short list of opinions, and there are only BUY recommendations, then do more research.
- If your analyst fails to provide perspective on a large portion of the industry covered, the information is incomplete and should be viewed with caution.
- If the entire list of stocks in an industry is long, but the analyst has opinions on only a few, it is fair to assume that they don't really like most of the stocks in the industry.
- If an analyst has BUY recommendations within an overall negatively-viewed industry, avoid the recommendations of the analyst within that industry. There is no reason to take the risk of buying stocks in negative industries.
- View neutral recommendations as sells.

In order to illustrate these points, look at the following Exhibits.

Exhibit 7-2
Oil Industry

Oil Company	Recommendation
Amerada Hess Corp.	Neutral
Anadarko Petroleum Corp.	Recommended
Apache Corp.	Recommended
Barrett Resources Corp.	Recommended
Basin Exploration Inc.	Buy
BP Amoco (ADR)	Recommended

Burlington Resources Inc.	Buy
Cabot Oil & Gas Corp.	Buy
Canadian Occidental Petroleum	Buy
Chevron Corp.	Buy
Conoco, Inc.	Neutral
Cross Timbers Oil Company	Buy
Devon Energy Corp.	Buy
EOG Resources Inc.	Recommended
Exxon Mobil Corp.	Recommended
Forcenergy Inc.	Buy
Forest Oil Corp.	Buy
The Houston Exploration Co.	Buy
Hugoton Royalty Trust	Buy
Kerr-McGee Corp.	Recommended
Meridian Resource Corp.	Buy
Mitchell Energy & Development	Trading Buy
Murphy Oil Corp.	Trading Buy
Newfield Exploration	Buy
Noble Affiliates, Inc.	Buy
Occidental Petroleum Corp.	Neutral
Ocean Energy, Inc.	Buy
Phillips Petroleum Company	Neutral
Pioneer Natural Resources Co.	Neutral
Pogo Producing Company	Recommended
Royal Dutch (U.S.)	Neutral
Shell T & T	Trading Buy
Texaco Inc.	Neutral
Tom Brown Inc.	Recommended
Union Pacific Resources	Recommended
Unocal Corp.	Recommended
USX-Marathon Group	Neutral
Vastar Resources	Recommended
Vintage Petroleum Inc.	Buy

17 Buy, 3 Trading Buy, 12 Recommended, 8 Neutral
Source: Goldman Sachs Americas Research: June 2000

Oil Industry — The analyst likes the oil industry. There are 17 buy recommendations, and only eight neutral (or sell) recommendations. Along with the ratings of trading buy and recommended (15), it is safe to assume that the industry is expected to do well. This is a clear case where the analyst is positive about the industry's prospects and believes most of the stocks will perform well.

Exhibit 7-3
Oil Services

Company	Recommendation
Baker Hughes Inc	Buy
BJ Services Co.	Trading Buy
Cooper Cameron Corp.	Buy
Diamond Offshort Drilling	Neutral
ENSCO International Inc.	Buy
Global Marine, Inc.	Recommended
Halliburton Company	Recommended
Hanover Compressor Company	Recommended
Louis Dreyfus Natural Gas Corp.	Buy
Marine Drilling Co.	Buy
Nabors Industries, Inc.	Buy
National-Oilwell, Inc.	Buy
Noble Drilling Corp.	Buy
PC Holdings (ADR)	Buy
Pride International	Buy
R & B Falcon	Buy
Rowan Companies, Inc.	Buy
Santa Fe International Corp.	Recommended
Schlumberger, Ltd.	Recommended
Smith International Inc.	Neutral
Veritas DGC Inc.	Buy

13 Buy, 1 Trading Buy, 5 Recommended, 2 Neutral
Source: Goldman Sachs Americas Research: June 2000

Oil Services — The analyst likes the oil services industry. There are 13 buy recommendations, 2 neutral (sell) recommendations, and 6 trading buy or recommended ratings. If the strategist recommends this industry, and relative strength confirms it, the oil services industry is a good one to consider for a stock portfolio, based upon the analyst's report.

Exhibit 7-4
Insurance

Company	Recommendation
ACE Limited	Buy
AFLAC Inc.	Recommended
Allmerica Financial Corp.	Buy
The Allstate Corp.	Recommended
American General Corp.	Buy
American International Group	Buy
AmerUS Life Holdings, Inc.	Buy
Aon Corp.	Neutral
AXA Financial Corp.	Recommended
E.W. Blanch Holdings, Inc.	Neutral
Chubb Corp.	Neutral
CAN Financial Corp.	Neutral
Conseco, Inc.	Neutral
Delphi Financial Group, Inc.	Buy
Everest Re Group Limited	Recommended
Fremont General Corp.	Neutral
The Hartford Financial Services	Recommended
HSB Group, Inc.	Neutral
Jefferson- Pilot Corp.	Neutral
John Hancock Financial	Recommended
Liberty Corp.	Neutral
Liberty Financial Companies	Neutral

Lincoln National Corp.	Neutral
March & McLennan Companies	Buy
MetLife Inc.	Recommended
The MONY Group	Buy
Mutual Risk Management Ltd.	Buy
Nationwide Financial Services, Inc.	Neutral
PartnerRE Ltd.	Buy
PAULA Financial	Neutral
The Progressive Corporation	Neutral
Protective Life Corp.	Neutral
Reinsurance Group of America	Buy
SAFECO Corp.	Neutral
St. Paul Companies	Neutral
StanCorp Financial Group, Inc.	Recommended
Torchmark Corp.	Neutral
Transatlantic Holdings, Inc.	Buy
Trenwick Group Inc.	Neutral
Unitrin, Inc.	Neutral
UnumProvident Corp.	Neutral
XL Capital Ltd.	Recommended

11 Buy, 10 Recommended, 21 Neutral
Source: Goldman Sachs Americas Research: June 2000

Insurance — The analyst is split on the insurance industry, with even recommendations for "buy" and "sell." Since the recommendations are split, it is important to investigate further before choosing a company from this industry. It could be that the analyst feels that some of the stocks have already performed well and met his price targets.

Exhibit 7-5
Computer Hardware

Company	Recommendation
ATI Technologies	Buy
Brocade Communications	Recommended
Cobalt Networks	Buy
EMC Corporation	Recommended
Hewlett-Packard Co.	Recommended
IKON Office Solutions	Neutral
International Business Machines	Recommended
Network Appliances, Inc.	Recommended
Silicon Graphics	Neutral
Storage Technology	Neutral
Sun Microsystems	Recommended
Tektronix, Inc.	Buy

3 Buy, 6 Recommended, 3 Neutral
Source: Goldman Sachs Americas Research: June 2000

Computer Hardware — The analyst is a little more positive about the computer hardware industry than the insurance industry, but the recommendations are three buys, three sells, and six recommended. Before choosing a company from the list, you should take a more careful look at the fundamentals of the stocks.

Exhibit 7-6
Consumer Cyclicals - Retail

Company	Recommendation
Abercrombie & Fitch	Neutral

The Use of the Analyst: The Third Opinion

AutoZone, Inc.	Buy
Barnes & Noble, Inc.	Buy
Bed, Bath & Beyond	Buy
Best Buy Company, Inc.	Buy
Borders Group, Inc.	Buy
Circuit City Stores, Inc.	Recommended
Consolidated Stores Corp.	Neutral
Costco Companies, Inc.	Neutral
Dillard Department Stores	Neutral
Distribution y Servicio (ADS)	Neutral
Dollar General Corp.	Recommended
Dollar Tree Stores, Inc.	Recommended
Family Dollar Stores, Inc.	Recommended
Federated Department Stores	Neutral
Finlay Enterprises, Inc.	Neutral
Gap, Inc.	Recommended
Group 1 Automotive, Inc.	Buy
Guitar Center, Inc.	Buy
Heilig-Meyers Company	Buy
The Home Depot, Inc.	Buy
Intimate Brands, Inc.	Recommended
Kmart Corp.	Neutral
Kohl's Corp.	Buy
Land's End, Inc.	Neutral
The Limited, Inc.	Buy
Liz Claiborne, Inc.	Recommended
The Lowe's Company, Inc.	Buy
The May Department Stores	Neutral
The Neiman Marcus Group	Neutral
99 Cents Only Stores	Buy
Nordstrom, Inc.	Neutral
Office Depot	Neutral
Office Max, Inc.	Buy
J.C. Penney Company	Neutral
Pep Boys	Neutral
RadioShack Corp.	Buy
Restoration Hardware	Neutral
Ross Stores, Inc.	Neutral
Saks, Inc.	Neutral

Sears, Roebuck, and Company	Neutral
Staples, Inc.	Recommended
Target Corporation	Buy
Tiffany & Company	Buy
The TJX Companies, Inc.	Neutral
Toys 'R Us, Inc.	Neutral
Trans World Corp.	Buy
Tuesday Morning Corp.	Buy
Wal-Mart de Mexico (ADR)	Buy
Wal-Mart Stores, Inc.	Buy
Williams-Sonoma, Inc.	Neutral
The Yankee Candle Company	Buy
Zale Corp.	Buy

23 Buy, 8 Recommended, 22 Neutral
Source: Goldman Sachs Americas Research: June 2000

Consumer Cyclicals (Retail) — The consumer cyclicals (retail) industry looks very similar to the computer hardware industry. Certain specialty retailers such as Barnes and Noble, Home Depot, and Bed Bath and Beyond look strong, but others like Lands End and Office Depot do not. The analyst's recommendations are positive, but once again, you must rely on picking stocks based on the fundamentals discussed at length in Chapter 8.

Exhibit 7-7
Banks

Company	Recommendation
AmSouth Bancorp	Neutral
Banco de Galicia	Buy
Banco Edwards (ADR)	Neutral
Banco Frances	Neutral

Banco Rio de la Plata	Neutral
Banco Santander Chile (ADR)	Neutral
Banco Santiago (ADR)	Neutral
Bac West Corp.	Buy
Bank of America Corporation	Recommended
BankOne Corp.	Trading Buy
BB&T Corp.	Buy
City National Corp.	Recommended
Comerica, Inc.	Recommended
Fifth Third Bancorp	Buy
First Midwest Bancorp Inc.	Recommended
First Tennessee National Corp.	Buy
First Union Corp.	Neutral
First Virginia Banks, Inc.	Neutral
Firstar Corporation	Recommended
FirstMerit Corp.	Buy
FleetBoston Financial Corp.	Buy
Huntington Bankshares Inc.	Neutral
KeyCorp	Buy
National City Corp.	Buy
North Fork Bancorp Inc.	Buy
PNC Financial Services Group	Buy
South Trust Corp.	Recommended
SunTrust Banks, Inc.	Recommended
Unibanco-Uniao de Bancos Bras.	Recommended List*
U.S. Bancorp	Trading Buy
Wachovia Corp.	Neutral
Wells Fargo & Company	Recommended
Westamerica Bancorporation	Buy
Zions Bancorporation	Recommended

12 Buy, 8 Recommended, 2 Trading Buy, 11 Neutral
Source: Goldman Sachs Americas Research: June 2000
*Recommended list for Latin America

Banks — The analyst is mixed on the banking industry, but a large number of the neutral (sell) recommenda-

tions are associated with international banks. With this industry, regional banks are more attractive candidates.

Exhibit 7-8
Outsourcing Services

Outsourcing Services	Quality	Recommendation
APAC	D	Recommended
Century Biz Svcs	D	Neutral
Cintas	B	Recommended
Franklin Covey	Review	
Interim Services	Review	
Kforce.com	Review	
Modis	Review	
ServiceMaster Co.	C	Neutral
SITEL Corp.	D	Recommended
Syke Enterprises	D	Neutral

Outsourcing Services — The outsourcing services industry includes only one "quality" company with a "B" rating. The rest of the companies have lower quality ratings. Notice that four companies are under review, and that the six companies rated are split evenly between sell and recommended ratings. This is an industry to avoid.

Notice that we are indicating that a neutral position on a stock is equivalent to a negative position. Analysts rate stocks with "buy," "accumulate," "neutral," "reduce" or "sell" opinions. In order to understand why we view any opinion "neutral" or lower as a "sell," understand that investors want their individual stock holdings to out-perform the market. No one deliberately selects a stock that is only expected to perform in-line with the market. If achieving market performance is the portfolio goal, then investors are better off buying index funds. If you invest in individual stocks, the goal is to identify stocks that will out-perform the market. We are likely to make enough mistakes by selecting just the best looking stocks. Thus, a neutral recommendation is equivalent to a sell recommendation from the viewpoint of trying to out-perform the market.

Troubleshooting: Analyst Coverage and Opinions

Analyst opinions vary dramatically. From one source to the next, you might see differences in the types and number of companies covered and/or the opinions on those companies. Depending upon your source, you are likely to find the following:

1. The analyst tries to cover a comprehensive list of companies in the industry, including large seasoned companies, small newer companies, companies that are high quality, more speculative companies, companies that are doing well, and those that are not. This type of coverage is by far the most useful. It provides a comprehensive view of the companies in the industry.
2. Other analysts have biases for small high growth companies or large seasoned ones. The list of stocks covered by these analysts may be less representational and reflect biases.
3. Some research departments' analysts only cover the stocks in the industries they like and provide

nothing on the industries they don't like. It is not unusual for a research department to eliminate research on entire industries that are out of favor at any point of time. Approaches like these are very confusing, because the analyst will provide coverage and then suddenly drop it. Additionally, the companies within the industries covered will change with their views. This type of research can cause the user to make many mistakes. If you see an analyst exhibit these patterns, find another primary source for analyst opinions. You may want to use this type of information as a secondary source.

4. Opinions are seldom consistent between analysts. One analyst may suggest a "strong buy" on almost every stock in the industry, akin to grade inflation at the universities. Another analyst may only recommend a "strong buy" on the very few, very best companies. Some analysts tend to always be bullish, while others are comfortable taking neutral stances, identifying only the best companies in their industries. Because of the inconsistencies with analysts, rely on other sources of research such as relative strength and strategist opinions.

Why are Analysts so Reluctant to Make Sell Recommendations?

Exhibit 7-9
Investment Recommendations
of Three Firms

	Buy	Accumulate	Neutral	Reduce
Firm A	351	493	319	5
Firm B	516	778	415	10
Firm C	147	559	332	6
	Positive		Negative	

Exhibit 7-9 shows how three major firms rate the stocks they follow. Notice that few sell recommendations are indicated, and that the worst third of all opinions are "neutral" or lower. The logical and correct conclusion is the neutral opinions are effectively sell opinions for the purposes of an individual investor building or managing her portfolio.

One of the more obvious reasons why analysts do not make many sell recommendations is that no one likes to make enemies, and telling the world to sell a company's stock is the worst of all possible insults to a company's management. Corporate America's executives do not take open criticism kindly. As a result, an analyst who tells the world to "sell" a company's stock is likely to face limited access to the company in the future. Information, once freely flowing between management and analyst, might be curtailed.

From an institutional perspective, the chance that the analyst's firm continues to be the investment banker for the company is severely limited as well. There are many articles about company executives becoming outraged about an analyst's "sell" opinion. The <u>Wall Street Journal</u> published an article on this subject titled "Analyst Feels Vindicated on Conseco" (April 14, 2000, p. C1), as did <u>Fortune</u> magazine ("The Price of Being Right," February 5, 2001, p. 128). In more than one case, the analyst is fired for negative recommendations on company stocks, yet securities firms insist the firings have nothing to do with the resulting problems between the company and the securities firm. Of course, these are isolated instances, and there are many cases where the analyst could not provide a positive recommendation and the firm's investment bankers passed on the opportunity to underwrite an offering.

The problem of potential conflicts of interest is in the news frequently. We saw it particularly in response to the persistent "buy" recommendations on Enron stock as the company was filing for Chapter 11 protection. In February 2002, the Securities and Exchange Commission considered new rulings to address the "conflict of interest" that analysts face. Analysts are employed by major financial institutions that have a stake in the companies that the analysts analyze. This fundamental problem with incentives isn't easily corrected. One suggestion, discussed in the business section of the <u>Los Angeles Times</u> (February 8, 2002), was to require that analysts recommendations be plotted against stock prices in analyst reports. With all of the recent publicity, new laws and changes in research department policies, analyst reports will probably become even better. Many of the new laws and policy changes work to remove pressure and conflicts of interest facing analysts.

It remains to be seen whether the practice of using "hold" or "neutral" recommendations to signal a "sell" opinions will continue. In the past, analysts put companies under review, or dropped coverage of stocks as a meaningful way to tell brokers and investors to sell. It is the investor's job to develop a discipline for investing that includes identifying and using these signals.

There has been tremendous controversy regarding the analyst's opinions. As a result, many of the major firms are simplifying their rating systems in order to make what they do more transparent to investors. Rather than the old system with five to six possible recommendations, many firms are going to a simpler, "buy/hold/sell" rating system. Another similar rating system would be "out-performing/market performance/under-performing." While reading analyst reports may be simpler with only three categories for recommendations, it remains to be seen what those categories will actually reflect. Analysts may or may not continue to over-weight "buy" recommendations, and the "hold" or "market performance" may end up reflecting a sell opinion. It will take several years before we will be able to clearly discern the analysts' intentions when they make recommendations. If analysts continue to face the same conflicts of interest that they have faced in the past, we will still need second and third opinions. Watching for changes in regulations surrounding the incentives facing analysts should provide insight. Further, researchers will study the distributions of analysts' recommendations as they have in the past. If the distributions heavily under-weight the "sell" recommendation within and across firms, then we know that "hold" or "market performance" will be "sell" recommendations.

Because of these changes, we cannot stress how important it is to use the multiple sources of information that we detail in this book. It is also imperative that investors use our final two steps in the process by examining the fundamental numbers and to finally study the company in detail. These two topics are discussed in detail in Chapter 8. In order to make the final buy and sell decisions about stocks, fundamental stock analysis is still the right end game. Other sources of information focus your search and alert you to major shifts in market sentiment. Remember that opinions are tools. In order to understand how to use the tool, you have to under-stand how it is intended to be used in order to achieve the desired results.

Conclusion

Use the reports of the securities analysts as a third step in the process of using securities research. If the strategist recommends an industry, and the relative strength charts confirm that the industry is on an upward trend, check the analyst's reports to see if the analyst has an overall positive view of the industry. Look for a ratio of at least three to two positive versus negative views. Remember that neutral does not mean neutral. Most of the time, a neutral rating is the worst rating an analyst will give to a company. Therefore, it should be considered a clear message to avoid the stock. Analyst's face strong pressures to present at least one buy recommendation in the industries that they are covering, and they often face conflicts of interest regarding the firms that they cover. For these reasons, use the analyst report as a check on other sources of data prior to proceeding to the specific analyses of the stocks.

Summary

Use a step-by-step screening of research information to find stocks for consideration.

1. Find a sector of the market that the strategist favors and recommends over-weighting.
2. Find an industry the strategist favors.
3. Find an industry that has a favorable relative strength trend.
4. Find an industry where the analyst has a majority of favorable recommendations, at least three to two.

When you complete each of these steps, it is appropriate to begin to evaluate individual stocks.

CHAPTER 8

Picking & Selling Individual Stocks

Market Indicators and Their Application to Stock Selection

In past chapters, we have taken you through a variety of steps toward creating a portfolio of stocks. After you have undertaken those steps you can focus upon stock selection.

Investors need criteria for screening companies. There is no optimal set of screening criteria, but each person should have some starting point for decision-making. There are generally five to 35 companies in each industry that an analyst will follow. Within the favored industries, more than half of those companies will have favorable ratings. You need a process for narrowing down the list of good companies to two or three stocks within a specific industry in order to focus on in-depth company research.

Implementing this process is made easier with the help of an advisor/partner. The following describes indicators that will help you and your financial advisor narrow the company list. Our list is a set that has worked well for many investors. As accounting practices and corporate governance rules change, new useful criteria will emerge, but this list provides a good starting point.

1. Quality. If the portfolio objective is conservative, only purchase high-quality stocks. In some cases, as with the Internet industry, there may not be blue chip-quality stocks. One should consider buying the highest-quality stocks available. Conversely, if the portfolio is aggressive, then both high quality and more speculative stocks can be considered. There is no reason why quality stocks cannot fulfill the needs of an aggressive portfolio — achieving outstanding returns without taking certain types of additional risk. S & P, Value Line or brokerage research analyst ratings are useful in determining the quality of individual stocks. One major source categorizes quality into the language of school children by giving stocks an "A," "B," "C" or "D" rating.

2. Look for stocks that have **higher earnings growth** rates than others in their industry, and more importantly, have been forecasted to maintain those higher rates for the next several years. Be sure to look at the last five years' earnings to check that the earnings growth is not just a recovery from several poor years' of earnings. It is important to know the quality of current and

future earnings growth. The Enron scandal certainly points to questionable accounting practices around reported earnings. Reform of accounting practices may lead analysts to look for better measures of profitability and projected growth.

3. Look for **value.** Price/earnings ratios that are lower than the industry may be one way to put value into industry perspective. However, absolute P/E ratios are of little interest if you are in the right industry. Evaluate P/E ratios relative to the rest of the industry. If the ratio is very low on a relative basis, it may indicate a problem with the firm. On the other hand, further research may indicate that the low relative P/E is screaming "BUY!" In certain industries where there are few present earnings, you may need to look to cash flows for an appropriate relative measure.

4. The "Peter Lynch system" or "PEG" ratio in which you look at the ratio of the P/E to earnings growth plus dividends is an excellent screen. This screen provides a value equalizer. If a stock is growing at 20 percent a year and selling at 20 times earnings, it is potentially a better value than a stock growing at 30 percent and selling at 40 times earnings.

5. Additional quantitative information can also be useful. The following are indicators that securities analysts and investors feel are important:

   a. Capitalization ratios or the size ranking within the industry — small firms often experience economic downturns more severely, but have a smaller base and can experience rapid growth.

149

b. Rate of return on equity gives a measure of the profitability in the business.

c. Dividend, dividend growth, and dividend payout if you are interested in dividends for your portfolio – these measures also provide a sense of the long-term liabilities of the firm.

d. Cash flow per share is often important for young, aggressive growth firms or firms with high start-up costs.

e. Beta is a measure of risk relative to the market/benchmark portfolio.

f. Long-term debt gives a sense of how highly leveraged the firm is. If a company has higher than industry debt levels, it should have higher than industry growth levels to show that the debt is being used effectively and that the company can service the debt.

g. Return on Equity (ROE) gives the investor a sense of the how much return is being provided relative to the shares outstanding.

Finally, once you narrow the list to a few stocks within a particular industry, study the individual companies. The numbers may look good, but if a company does not make sense to you, or you just don't have a good feel for the company, you may want to pass on that stock and continue your search. The company should have a compelling story that makes sense. It is very important to have a good understanding of an industry and company in order to make good decisions regarding the stock after you own it.

Buy and Sell Disciplines Between Financial Advisors and Investors

In order to communicate effectively, advisors and investors must use a systematic approach to stock selection that is logical for both the advisor and the investor. In each step of portfolio management, the burden is on the advisor to communicate simply and clearly with the investor about the procedures being used. The most productive way to communicate is to develop disciplines for decision-making. Communication will improve dramatically if disciplines are developed. As in any team effort, a successful investment experience involves both members of the team. Most important decisions are made during confusing investment environments, so having disciplines in place is very important. One of the most beneficial things an advisor can do for an investor is to stop him from making foolish decisions, and vice versa.

The following is one example of a set of buy disciplines that help the advisor and the investor work together effectively. It is very important for advisors and investors to establish rules for buying and selling stocks. These rules are particularly important when an investor is facing selling stock at a loss. By having disciplines regarding buying and selling, investors will be able to make better decisions during stressful situations.

Suggested Buy Disciplines

1. Select stocks that fit the overall portfolio strategy.
2. Focus research on stocks that are in the sectors and industries of the market that our investment strategist strongly favors.
3. Of those industries, select only those industries

that have strong price performance relative to the market, or have bottomed-out and have started to show strong sign of recovery.

4. Any industry must have a preponderance of "buy" opinions by the industry analyst. Do not consider purchase of a company's stock in an industry unless the analyst likes the industry overall. (The only exception to this discipline is when one must diversify a portfolio to move it in line with the benchmark and there are generally negative views on the sector.)

5. All of the companies considered will have a buy recommendation from the analyst.

6. All of the companies considered will meet high-quality standards, given the overall quality of the industry.

7. Select stocks with earnings or cash flows that are growing faster than those in its industry.

8. Select stocks that have relatively low valuations within their industry.

9. Select stocks that have an interesting story that we can understand and appreciate.

The best part of having disciplines is that you can disregard 90 percent of all research available and screen to concentrate on the right stocks. It is impossible to read everything and then decide what is or is not useful without some filtering process. The only way to focus on important information is to have a clear idea of what not to read. At the same time, you will need sources of information to identify trends. In order to be efficient, you must have good monitoring tools and resources in place so that you can spend a few hours each month checking the overall picture. When new trends appear, you want enough lead-time and a plan to confirm the changes.

Individual brokers and investors may modify the above disciplines to fit their styles, but the limiting rule is that the criteria should be logical, decision specific and easy to use. The above buy disciplines meet the criteria, and can be easily monitored.

As an example of using this disciplined buy process, we take you through an analyst report for the retail drug industry for 2002.

Exhibit 8-1
Retail Drugs

Company	Quality	Opinion	Earnings Per Share			P/E Multiple		P/E Relative to Market
			Last Year Actual	Current Year Est.	Next Year Est.	This Year	Next Year	
CVS Corp	Speculative	Buy	1.57	4.69	1.92	16.50	14.50	0.58
Duane Reade	Speculative	Buy	1.23	1.23	1.78	21.80	15.10	0.77
Rite Aid	H Risk	Hold	1.97d	0.77d	0.38d	NM	NM	nil
Walgreen	H Quality	Buy	0.85	1.00	1.20	37.90	31.50	1.33
Composite			1.00	1.18	1.41	33.00	27.50	1.16

Company	Earnings Per Share Growth				Beta Coefficient	ROE	L.T. Liab. % of Cap.
	Last 5 Years	Last Year	Current Year	Next 5 Years			
CVS Corp	NA	8.00	14.00	14	0.68	20	19
Duane Reade	NA	0.00	45.00	18	0.16	25	48
Rite Aid	NA	nm	nm	nm	0.45	nm	63
Walgreen	18.00	18.00	20.00	20	0.7	19	11
Composite	18.00	16.00	19.00	19	0.68	19	15

Walgreen is the one company rated as high quality. All of the rest of the companies are either speculative or high risk. The analyst also has a buy recommendation on Walgreen. The other company that is interesting is speculative, but given the fact that there is only one company of high quality, it is worth looking at another company in the industry. Duane Reade looks interesting, in spite of its speculative rating.

Walgreen is forecast to grow at 20 percent for the next five years, just above the 19 percent rate for the industry. The earnings growth has been consistently high for the last five-year period of time. The current earnings are strong and forecasted to be high next year. Walgreen is selling at a 37.9 P/E ratio for this year and 31.5 for next years projected earnings. This is a premium to the 33.0 and 27.5 for the industry, and also a premium to the market. With only three companies with numbers to forge a composite, the numbers are not that statistically significant within the industry, however. Walgreen has P/E ratios that are 30 percent above the industry and slightly above the S & P market P/E ratio. The PEG ratios are just above the industry PEG ratio for this year but just below the industry for the next year. Walgreen has a .70 Beta, an industry average 19 percent ROE and below 11 percent capitalization rate. Walgreen is a company that should be included in the portfolio, in spite of its premium price and P/E ratio, after review of a detail research report on the company.

Duane Reade is a speculative-rated company and is forecast to grow at an 18 percent rate for the next five years. This company does not have a historical five-year record. Duane Reade's P/E ratios are 21.8 for this year and 15.1 for next year. This combination of P/E ratios and growth rates yield PEG ratios of 1.2 versus 1.8 for the industry for this year and 0.8 for next year. The industry average for next year is 1.4. These numbers place a very interesting valuation on the company. The lack of five years of earnings in this report requires that detailed information regarding the company is necessary. Duane Reade is interesting based upon the existing numbers. Its P/E ratio based on next year's projected earnings growth is below its growth rate. This is a good measure of a reasonable valuation for the company.

When undertaking this type of review, if you are missing key information, Value Line research service is an excellent source of needed historic information and company descriptions.

After you have completed the process of using the market indicators, examine the full research report of the analysts on the companies identified and any additional research such as annual reports that you need to address any concerns. Please note that even if you read the full analyst report, you may still receive a biased view about the company if the analyst is facing strong conflicts of interest. Because analysts are currently under such scrutiny by the SEC and other investigatory agencies, we feel that analyst reports remain a good source of information for the investor. There are thousands of practicing securities analysts. While some analysts have made poor recommendations to investors in recent years, it does not mean that all analysts are corrupt. Only a few analysts faced serious questions about their integrity during the crises of 2002. The new laws and company policies will likely improve the quality of the analyst's reports.

When reading individual company research reports, you will know why the company has been selected and what questions you are trying to answer. Your research will be focused and you will decrease the amount of time spent with irrelevant research.

On the other side of the decision-making process, the best advisors and investors have a set of sell disciplines. A common experience for an advisor is when an investor says "I don't need help with choosing stocks, but I do need help knowing when to sell." Sell decisions are difficult for advisors and portfolio managers, and are made even more difficult when the recommendation is that an investor sell at a loss. By having an agreed discipline regarding selling, the decision process and discussion surrounding it is much easier. Further, the investor will be much more willing to take advice.

Too often both advisors and investors are tempted to sell winning stocks and hold losers. A tax-efficient and effective strategy is to do just the opposite, yet often profits are cut short and losses are allowed to run. The reason that sell decisions are important is that they control losses. Look at the law of numbers in Exhibit 8-2. It makes the point clear about why controlling losses is so important.

Exhibit 8-2
The First Law of Numbers

% Decline in Stock Price	% Gain in Stock Price (to Break Even from Decline)
10%	11%
25%	33%
50%	100%
75%	400%

The law of numbers represents a mathematical truth and it points to an important investing principle – good investing means avoiding big losses, and taking advantage of the tax breaks associated with losses. If a stock price falls by half, or goes from $100 to $50, the price must double in order to get back to $100 again. In percentage terms, you need a 100 percent gain to make up for the loss. The percentage gains increase dramatically with the size of the loss, so a 75 percent loss on one stock will require a 400 percent gain in a stock of equal value in order for the portfolio to break even. Taking losses strategically can offset capital gains, increasing after-tax returns. The best sell practice is to cut losses short and let profits run, that is if you have credible research to support that the stock will continue to be profitable. Keep winning stocks and sell losers to make more money over the long run.

Each month, investors receive statements that show the cost and current market price of each security owned. Realized profits or losses generally do not appear on the statement. The statement alters the perception of how the portfolio is doing by maintaining positions in losing stocks. It is not a good practice for the investor to take short-term profits and leave the remaining portfolio with significant losses versus the purchase price, because it may alter the perception about the team's effectiveness. Sell disciplines help to avoid these problems, and are generally the reverse of buy disciplines, with a few exceptions.

Suggested Sell Disciplines

1. If the investment strategist makes a change from over-weighting to market-weighting or under-

weighting a sector of the market, consider moving the money to a more favorable sector.

2. If the relative strength for a selected industry turns negative, consider selling securities in that group, or at least decrease the commitment. Move the money to a more favorable industry.

3. If the industry analyst has more unfavorable than favorable opinions on stocks in the industry they are covering, consider selling — even if the analyst maintains a good opinion of the individual stock in the portfolio.

4. If the analyst downgrades his recommendation of the stock to neutral or lower, SELL.

5. If the analyst lowers earnings estimates twice, sell regardless of other recommendations. Remember that there is no such thing as one bad quarter.

6. If the analyst drops his recommendation, sell. Do not fly blind or try to become the analyst.

7. If the forecasted earnings growth slows to less than the industry average, consider selling.

8. If the P/E ratio or "Peter Lynch ratio" exceeds the industry by a significant amount, consider selling. The future price appreciation is likely to slow.

9. If there is significant bad news, sell and take another look to see if the stock is the best place to be invested. If the stock is still a good investment, the cost of two commissions is very little compared to large losses.

10. If an investment reaches your three-year price target in less than 18 months, consider selling. There is little price appreciation left for the next few years.

Conclusion

Put in place a set of buy and sell disciplines to support stock purchases and sales. Use this process only after thinking about the needs of the overall portfolio. Look to the sectors and industries prior to stock selection. Then carefully use market indicators and company annual reports to make your decisions.

CHAPTER 9

Creating a Stock Portfolio from Scratch

Putting it All Together to Create
a Winning Portfolio

In previous chapters, we discussed an approach to building portfolios. In this chapter, we will walk through the steps to build a stock portfolio utilizing the major securities research sources, and discussing each one in detail. For ease and simplicity of explanation, we will focus on only two S & P 500 sectors. The same process would be used on all 10 S & P 500 sectors if you were to build a stock portfolio from scratch. We emphasize the U.S. market because of its complexity and ease of access to quality research materials.

Before we get started, we need to discuss a significant issue that arises when applying the approach. When putting a portfolio together with research from a variety of sources, there will be some problems and inconsistencies. Because businesses and industries evolve over time with the development of new products, technological developments and management practices, the manner in which researchers characterize industries necessarily has to change over time. One example is when the S & P made major changes to their industry classifications in 2002. The old classification standards no longer adequately explained differences and similarities in firms, industries and sectors, so S & P undertook a major reclassification. Their new "Global Industry Classification Standards" (GICS) are available on their Web site (*www.standardandpoors.com*). When one research source makes major changes, other research sources may take some time to catch up — or worse, they might choose to use another classification standard.

Specifically, market strategists don't necessarily use the S & P 500 classification standards, and generally speaking, classification standards vary across firms. Worse than the problems across firms, even within firms analysts and strategists often disagree about industry classifications. As a result, the "science" of portfolio construction involves quite a bit of creative work. Like so many other industries, the securities industry would do a great favor to investors if all of their research classifications were brought into compliance with Standard & Poor's GICS. Strategists and analysts could easily add any modifications that they believed added clarity to the classifications. Such clarity would increase the value of their research products to all users.

The use of securities research described in this book is thus a combination of science and art. As we construct the examples in this chapter, we will follow the steps discussed in early chapters, but things will get a little messy and require some interpretation in applying a discipline to using securities research. The examples we use will provide evidence of these problems. For example, the strategist we used places the biotechnology industry in the consumer staples sector. The S & P GICS places biotechnology in the healthcare sector, creating a bit of confusion when the researcher searches for the biotechnology relative and absolute strength data. Other potential problems have to do with major disagreements across the research sources about the performance of the industries. We will define and discuss the conflicts in classifications when they occur, and provide information about how to resolve the conflicts across sources.

The box below summarizes the steps we will discuss by example in this chapter.

Steps to Using Securities Research

1. *Asset Allocation:* Make asset allocation choices based upon your risk tolerance, age and personal needs. The longer the time horizon until you need access to the funds, the more heavily weighted you should be in stocks. Check bi-annually to see if allocation *target* percentages match *actual* allocation percentages.
2. *Benchmark and Portfolio Style and Objectives:* Identify your investing style and objectives. How do you want to enhance returns above your benchmark? Do you want

---

a more aggressive portfolio that is more risky — earning potentially higher returns? If so, then you'll want to construct a portfolio with a slightly higher beta. Do you want a portfolio mainly comprised of "small cap" stocks? If so, then you'll want to maintain your sector and industry weightings, but build the portfolio with stocks from smaller, less known companies. We recommend a sector-neutral, fully-invested approach with a few modifications to enhance performance, or to gain alpha beyond the benchmark for your portfolio style. Remember, depending upon your needs, you can take a more conservative approach or one that is substantially more aggressive.

3. *Investment Strategist:* Assess the market by using an investment strategist's sector and industry analysis. Once you decide which strategy to pursue, you can either use the chosen strategist's recommendations of over and under-weighting sectors, or you can use a sector-neutral approach and focus research efforts on the recommended industries, choosing the best stocks in the favored industries. The strategist will have different weightings for the sectors and industries, depending upon the portfolio style and objectives.

4. *Relative Strength:* After having identified several industries recommended by the

strategist, use relative strength charts to check whether the industries are in favor in the market. Check for a confirmed upward trend or identify industries that have bottomed-out and are beginning to recover.

5. *Analyst Appraisal of Industry:* Having narrowed the list of industries, get a third opinion from the analyst. Check the analyst ratings for the entire industry. If there is only one or a small percentage of stocks that the analyst favors, the industry is not expected to perform well in the near future. Remember that neutral recommendations are sell recommendations.

6. *Individual Companies:* Survey individual stocks in selected industries according to pre-established criteria such as quality, growth rate, P/E ratios, PEG ratios, dividends, dividend growth, book value, return on equity, capitalization ratios, etc. Compare these criteria to those of the composite for the industry. Remember to compare the fundamental screens within the industry and not necessarily with the market as a whole.

7. *Selecting Stocks:* After identifying several stocks in each industry you are considering, analyze each company in depth with detailed analyst reports and the company's annual report. The company's story, which must pass your screen, is provided in the annual report.

The consumer staples sector has few inconsistencies across research sources, and provides a good example of how to implement the process. We will start with this sector. The second example we discuss, capital goods-technology, provides more challenges. We will use the capital goods-technology sector to discuss more of the art of putting it all together.

Putting it all Together

The first step for any investor in building a portfolio is to make asset allocation decisions based upon your risk tolerance, age and personal needs. This topic is discussed at length in Chapter 3. The next step involves setting a benchmark.

Strategists' reports provide recommendations for different styles and objectives. The objectives can vary from "the preservation of capital" to "aggressive growth." For the purposes of this example, we chose a style and objective for the portfolio. Remember that each individual must make policy decisions appropriate to his needs, risk tolerance and style preferences, carefully considering the particular point in history for the market and his goals. The policy decision we made was to construct a "conservative growth" portfolio. We are not recommending this portfolio objective. We are simply using this portfolio objective as an example. We do not have a particular preference regarding market capitalization, only that the stock is listed on an exchange such as NYSE, NASDAQ or other exchanges that have minimal listing and disclosure standards.

After choosing your investment style, examine the strategist's complete set of recommendations for

sectors and industries. We used recommendations from
February 2002. If we had started the process in 1997, we
might have created quite a different looking portfolio.
In the interest of simplicity, Exhibit 9-1 provides a
summary of the recommended portfolio weightings for
two of the sectors and industries for a "conservative
growth" portfolio. Our strategist recommendations are
based upon those of major securities firms. A full set
of recommendations for all sectors and industries can
be found from large securities firms and are usually
published quarterly. Exhibit 9-1 includes the portfolio
weightings for the S & P 500 benchmark and for
two other objectives for comparison, "growth" and
"aggressive growth." Note that the "+" signs are used to
highlight the favored industries within the sector.

Exhibit 9-1
Strategist's Recommendations
for Three Portfolio Styles

Sector	S & P 500	Conservative Growth	Growth	Aggressive Growth
Consumer Staples	22.00%	22.00%	21.00%	20.00%
Pharmaceuticals		"+"	"+"	"+"
Medical Technology		"+"	"+"	"+"
Long-term Care		"+"	"+"	"+"
Foods		"+"		
Beverage-Soft Drink		"+"		
Beverage-Brewers/Distillers		"+"		
Household Products		"+"		
Cosmetics & Personal Care		"+"	"+"	
Food and Drug Retailers		"+"	"+"	
Biotechnology			"+"	"+"
Tobacco				

167

Sector	S & P 500	Conservative Growth	Growth	Aggressive Growth
Capital Goods-Technology	22.00%	15.00%	26.00%	32.00%
Computer Services		"+"	"+"	"+"
Electronics/Conductors		"+"	"+"	"+"
Server Hardware & Appliances		"+"	"+"	"+"
Personal Computer Hardware				
Computer Software			"+"	"+"
Internet Software & Services			"+"	"+"
Imaging Equipment				
Electronics-Semiconductors			"+"	"+"
Electronics - Semiconductor Capital Equip.			"+"	"+"
Telecommunications Equipment		"+"		
Telecommunications Satellite				
Telecommunications Network			"+"	"+"
Telecommunications - Long Distance		"+"		
Telecommunications - Wireless Services		"+"		
Energy Technology				"+"

The consumer staples sector has a large weight in the portfolio of 22 percent. We want to place that proportion of our dollar investments into the consumer staples sector in order to be both sector neutral and to meet the strategist's recommendations. The strategist has recommended all of the industries but the biotechnology and tobacco industries for an "income & growth" objective. He recommends under-weighting the capital goods-technology sector to 15 percent, and recommends six industries.

The next step in the process of using securities research is to check these recommendations against the relative strength charts. Relative strength gives another perspective about these sectors. Our source for relative and absolute strength data is *www.quantumrelativestrength.com*. It provides charts of market trends from 1990 to present. The following charts show both the absolute and relative price performance for the consumer staples sector and several of its associated industries.

Exhibit 9-2
Consumer Staples Sector

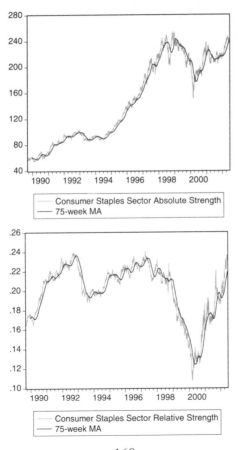

169

The consumer staples sector is in an upward trend, reinforcing the strategist's recommendation for over-weighting it. Two industries within the sector — pharmaceuticals and food retail — show volatility during 2002 with possible "bearish" tendencies. The other industries in the sector show positive relative strength.

Exhibit 9-3
Selected Industry Relative Strength
Charts for Consumer Staples

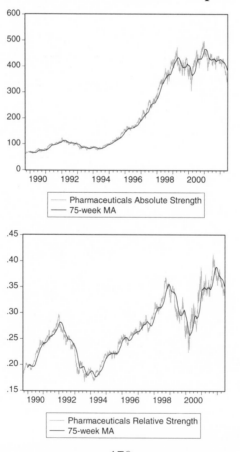

Food Retail Absolute Strength ——— 75-week MA

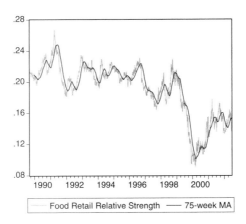

Food Retail Relative Strength ——— 75-week MA

As examples of positive industries, see the soft drinks and health care facilities industries.

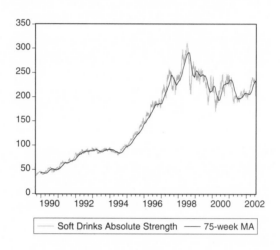

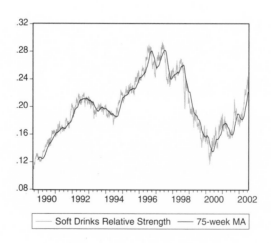

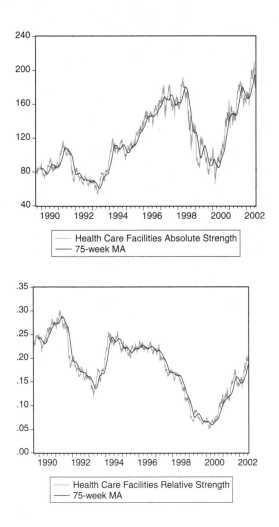

⋯⋯⋯	Health Care Facilities Absolute Strength
——	75-week MA

——	Health Care Facilities Relative Strength
——	75-week MA

A Note About the Charts

Some of the industry names differ in the relative strength charts from the industries listed in Exhibit 9-1. Because the relative strength charts are based upon the GICS and the strategist's classifications are not, there are slight differences. For example, the foods industry is actually in two charts, foods distributors and packaged foods. The medical technology sector is the healthcare equipment sector according to the GICS. The differences can be easily reconciled by going to Standard and Poor's Web site and examining the individual companies within the industries. It takes a little extra effort, but with experience it is simple. Exhibit 9-4 is an example of how we linked the graphs to the strategist's recommendations. This exhibit shows how the strategist's sector groupings map to relative strength classifications.

Exhibit 9-4
Strategist vs. Relative Strength
Classifications

Strategist	Relative Strength
Pharmaceuticals	Pharmaceuticals
Medical Technology	Healthcare Equipment
Long-term Care	Healthcare Facilities
Foods	Food Distributors
	Packaged Foods
Beverage - Soft Drink	Soft Drinks
Beverage - Brewers/Distiller	Brewers
Household Products	Household Products
Cosmetics & Personal Care	Personal Products
Food and Drug Retailers	Food Retail
Biotechnology	Biotechnology
Tobacco	Tobacco

In summary, a survey of the industries shows that most of the recommended industries in the consumer staples sector are displaying positive relative strength.

There is almost complete confirmation for the strategist's industry recommendations, providing confidence about our focus on this sector and on the recommended industries.

The fifth step in our process is to get a third opinion on the industries that we want to examine more closely by inspecting industry analyst's reports. We want to see if the analyst likes the majority of stocks in the industry. We used one large security brokerage's research as the basis for our examples provided in Exhibits 9-5 through 9-7 and for the other industries summarized in this section. Exhibit 9-5 shows the analyst's recommendations for the healthcare facilities industry, Exhibit 9-6 shows the recommendations for the soft drinks industry and Exhibit 9-7 provides the recommendations for the pharmaceuticals industry. We summarize the results for the other industries in the consumer staples sector below.

Exhibit 9-5
Analyst's Recommendations
Healthcare Facilities

Company	Quality	Recommend.
Community Health	Speculative	S Buy
HCA	Speculative	S Buy
Health Mgt Assoc.	Speculative	S Buy
LifePoint	Speculative	S Buy
Province Health	Speculative	S Buy
Quorum Health	RSTR	
Tenet Healthcare	G Quality	S Buy
Triad Hospitals	Speculative	S Buy

Company	Quality	Recommend.
Univ Health Svcs	Speculative	S Buy
Beverly Enterprises	Speculative	Neutral
Manor Care	Speculative	S Buy
Sunrise	H Risk	Neutral
Genesis Health	Review	

Healthcare Facilities: The analyst follows 13 stocks and has opinions on 11 of them. He has very positive opinions on nine companies and neutral opinions on the other two stocks. The analyst likes this industry overall. We have positive confirmation about this industry from three sources.

Exhibit 9-6
Analyst's Recommendations
Soft Drinks Industry

Company	Quality	Recommend.
Coca-Cola	H Quality	Buy
Coca-Cola Bottling	Speculative	S Buy
Coca-Cola Ent	Speculative	Buy
Pepsi Bottling	Speculative	Neutral
PepsiAmericas	Speculative	Neutral
PepsiCO	H Quality	Buy
Cott Corp	High Risk	S Buy

Soft Drinks: The analyst has opinions on seven companies in the soft drink industry. Two of the companies are the major soft drink companies and the rest are bottlers and distributors. The analyst rates two companies as strong buys, three as buys and two as neutral. The analyst likes this industry overall. We have positive confirmation about this industry from the strategist, relative strength and the analyst.

Exhibit 9-7
Analyst's Recommendations
Pharmaceuticals Industry

Company	Quality	Recommend.
Allergan	G Quality	S Buy
American Home	G Quality	Buy
Andrx Corp	H Risk	S Buy
Bristol Meyers	H Quality	S Buy
Forest Labs	G Quality	Buy
Heska Corp	High Risk	Neutral
IVAX Corp	Speculative	Neutral
King Pharma	Speculative	Buy
Lilly	G Quality	Buy
Merck	H Quality	Neutral
Mylan Labs	RVW	
Pfizer	H Quality	S Buy
Pharmacia	G Quality	S Buy
SangStat	H Risk	Buy
Schering	H Quality	Buy
Sepracor	H Risk	Buy
SICOR	H Risk	S Buy
Watson Pharm	Speculative	Buy

Pharmaceuticals Industry: The analyst has opinions on 17 stocks in the pharmaceuticals industry. He has positive recommendations on 14 of them. The recommendations are six strong buys, eight buys and three neutrals. Using our approach of lining up all three sources of information we find that while the strategist and analyst like the industry, the relative strength does not confirm their views. The question we must ask is "What should we do about this industry?"

In the case where one of our screening sources disfavors an industry, we need to assess how big a problem we would have with risk management if we were to exclude the industry from the portfolio. In the case of the pharmaceuticals industry, it represents 10 percent of the entire S & P 500. We probably do not want to exclude it from the portfolio because doing so represents too big a deviation from the benchmark. Because two of our screens favor the industry, we will proceed forward with this industry, but we will proceed with caution. In adding pharmaceutical stocks to the portfolio, we suggest using a dollar cost averaging approach and slowly accumulating the stock over time. Dollar cost averaging is explained in detail in Chapter 10.

Cosmetics and Personal Care: The industry analyst has three of the stocks under review. There are no strong buys, two buys and five neutral recommendations. The analyst's favorite is Estee-Lauder. The company is growing faster than the industry, but has a very high P/E ratio. Avoid this industry at this time, since there are more attractive options in other industries in the sector.

Food Retail Industry: The food retail industry report shows that the analyst is not very positive on the industry. There are 10 companies covered in this industry, and the analyst has a positive recommendation on four of the 10 companies. Specifically, there are two strong buys, two buys, four neutrals and four sells. With a negative bias toward the industry, one should look to other industries within the sector.

Foods: There are 10 companies examined in the processed foods industry. Five are buys, and five are neutral. Within the foods distributors industry, there are six companies covered, five are buys and one is neutral. The weight of the overall foods industry is positive, with the emphasis on the distributors industry.

Medical Technology Industry: Here we have many companies to choose from, the analyst covers 22 companies. There are six strong buys, 11 buys, three neutrals and three companies under review. We have all three research sources positive on the industry, and a rich group of stocks from which to choose.

Household Products Industry: The analyst is covering eight companies. Two companies are under review and the remaining six companies have four buy recommendations and two neutral recommendations. There are no strong buy recommendations. These recommendations provide a favorable bias for the industry, but this is not a screaming endorsement. The industry looks okay, but not great.

Drug Retail Industry: The drug retail industry has only four companies covered by the analyst, none of which has a strong buy recommendation. There are three buy recommendations and one neutral. Between the food and drug retail industries there are seven buys and seven sells. There is enough evidence to go forward to find one or two attractive stocks for the portfolio. Caution is warranted since we do not have broad coverage here. If one feels that bringing in some stocks in this area would help provide diversification to the portfolio, there is enough evidence to go forward with one or two stocks.

There are better retail opportunities in other sectors of the S & P, however.

Summarizing, an investor should research stocks in the following industries: soft drink, health care facilities, pharmaceuticals and medical technology industries, based upon the evidence provided by the strategist, relative strength and analyst reports.

The sixth step in the research involves examining specific indicators about the stocks within our chosen industries. We highlight the soft drinks, health care facilities and pharmaceuticals industries for illustration. Exhibit 9-8 provides a list of market indicators for the soft drinks industry.

We suggest the criteria for selecting individual stocks are the following: higher quality (especially for a conservative growth portfolio), good analyst recommendations, growth rates that are faster than the industry average, a lower P/E ratio than the industry average and PEG ratio approaching one. Given these criteria, there is one company that stands out in the **soft drink industry**. PepsiCo is a high quality company. It has a buy rating from the analyst, has consistent earnings growth and is expected to grow at a significantly higher rate than the industry. It is selling at a bit higher P/E ratio than the industry, has a beta of .70 that is about in line with the industry, a good ROE and a much lower long-term liability than the industry. After reading detailed research reports on the company, it will most likely be a strong candidate for the portfolio.

Selected Market Indicators

Quality: Choose the highest quality possible. Quality is especially important for a conservative portfolio objective.

Earnings Growth: Look for higher than industry average rates of growth. Be careful that the present higher earnings growth is not due to lower than average growth in past years.

Value: Identify stocks with lower P/E ratios, considering their quality within the industry. Another consideration is the company's P/E ratio, relative to the overall market P/E.

P/E to growth or PEG: Identify stocks with earnings growth greater than what is reflected in the price to earnings ratio.

Capitalization ratios: There are shifts in popularity and performance of portfolios of different capitalization ratios. Sometimes "small cap" outperform "large cap" and sometimes vice versa.

Rate of return on equity: Gives a measure of the profitability of the business.

Dividends and dividend growth: If you are interested in dividends, you will want to take a hard look at these numbers. If you are interested in growth stocks, you may want to avoid stocks with high dividends.

Cash flow per share: Examine this number when looking at small or rapidly growing companies.

Beta: This measure is a basic indicator of the stock's risk relative to the market.

Long-term debt: Debt levels can be high or low for quality firms, depending upon how they are using the money. Borrowing for expansion is often important.

Exhibit 9-8
Analyst Recommendations and Market Indicators
Soft Drink Industry

Company	Quality	Opinion	Earnings Per Share			P/E Multiple		P/E Relative to Market
			Last Year Actual	Current Year Est.	Next Year Est.	This Year	Next Year	
Coca-Cola	H Quality	Buy	1.60	1.80	2.00	32.0	28.5	1.2
Coca-Cola Bottling	Speculative	S Buy	0.75	2.40	2.90	20.8	17.2	0.8
Coca-Cola Ent	Speculative	Buy	-0.05	0.70	0.90	28.5	22.2	1.1
Pepsi Bottling	Speculative	Neutral	0.95	1.45	1.65	20.4	17.9	0.8
PepsiAmericas	Speculative	Neutral	0.58	1.00	1.10	15.2	13.8	0.6
PepsiCo	H Quality	Buy	1.66	1.95	2.15	27.0	24.6	1.1
Cott Corp	High Risk	S Buy	0.58	0.75	1.00	26.6	20.0	1.0
Composite			0.87	1.44	1.67	24.36	20.60	0.95

Exhibit 9-8
Analyst Recommendations and Market Indicators — Con't
Soft Drink Industry

	Earnings Per Share Growth				Beta Coefficient	ROE	L.T. Liab. % of Cap.
	Last 5 Years	Last Year	Current Year	Next 5 Years			
Coca-Cola	3	13	11	5	0.85	35	9
Coca-Cola Bottling	-15	220	21	5	0.30	55	90
Coca-Cola Ent	na	nm	28	9	0.75	23	57
Pepsi Bottling	16	50	14	16	0.80	22	60
PepsiAmericas	-15	84	10	9	0.80	10	33
PepsiCO	8	17	10	12	0.70	32	18
Cott Corp	7	29	33	7	0.75	23	57
Composite	*1.00*	*59*	*18*	*9*	*0.71*	*29*	*46*

Exhibit 9-9
Analyst Recommendations and Market Indicators
Healthcare Facilities Industry

| Company | Quality | Opinion | Earnings Per Share | | | P/E Multiple | | P/E Relative |
			Last Year Actual	Current Year Est.	Next Year Est.	This Year	Next Year	to Market
Community Health	Speculative	S Buy	0.54	0.93	1.12	30.1	25	0.7
HCA	Speculative	S Buy	1.94	2.41	2.8	18.8	16.2	0.44
Health Mgt Assoc.	Speculative	S Buy	0.8	0.96	1.12	20.8	17.8	0.48
LifePoint	Speculative RSTR	S Buy	0.93	1.3	1.6	29.4	23.9	0.68
Quorum Health								
Tenet Healthcare	G Quality	S Buy	2.3	3.2	4.1	22.4	17.4	0.52
Triad Hospitals	Speculative	S Buy	0.61	1.7	2.05	24	19.9	0.56
Beverly Enterprises	Speculative	Neutral	0.44	0.54	0.45	15.4	18.5	0.36
Manor Care	Speculative	S Buy	1.15	1.33	1.45	19.2	17.7	0.45
Sunrise	H Risk	Neutral	1.96	2.27	2.57	12	10.6	0.28
Genesis Health	Review							
Composite			1.17	1.69	1.88	20.5	18.6	0.48

Exhibit 9-9

Analyst Recommendations and Market Indicators — Con't

Healthcare Facilities Industry

	Earnings Per Share Growth				Beta Coefficient	ROE	L.T. Liab. % of Cap.
	Last 5 Years	Last Year	Current Year	Next 5 Years			
Community Health	na	72	20	25	0.14	5	20
HCA	-5	24	16	15	0.68	20	17
Health Mgt Assoc.	19	20	17	15	0.83	17	17
LifePoint	na	40	23	25	0.39	16	10
Quorum Health							
Tenet Healthcare	2	39	28	15	0.56	15	45
Triad Hospitals	na	179	21	18	na	1	50
Beverly Enterprises	na	23	-17	10	0.9	nm	55
Manor Care	-12	16	9	15	1.05	7	40
Sunrise	na	16	13	na	na	na	59
Genesis Health							
Composite	*1.72*	*58*	*9.4*	*16*	*0.53*	*9*	*30*

Exhibit 9-10
Analyst Recommendations and Market Indicators
Pharmaceuticals Industry

Company	Quality	Opinion	Earnings Per Share			P/E Multiple		P/E Relative
			Last Year Actual	Current Year Est.	Next Year Est.	This Year	Next Year	to Market
Allergan	G Quality	S Buy	1.96	2.36	2.83	29.6	24.7	1.04
American Home	G Quality	Buy	2.18	2.61	3.00	24.3	21.1	0.85
Andrx Corp	H Risk	S Buy	1.05	1.07	3.00	43.4	15.5	1.53
Bristol Meyers	H Quality	S Buy	2.41	2.29	2.58	19.8	17.6	0.70
Forest Labs	G Quality	Buy	1.18	1.79	2.16	45.5	37.5	1.60
Heska Corp	High Risk	Neutral	0.63d	0.42d	0.19	dnm	Nm	nm
IVAX Corp	Speculative	Neutral	0.94	1.10	ne	15.9	Na	0.56
Lilly	G Quality	Buy	2.75	2.69	3.14	28.2	24.1	0.99
Merck	H Quality	Neutral	3.14	3.14	3.47	19.2	17.4	0.67
Mylan Labs	RVW							
Pfizer	H Quality	S Buy	1.31	1.61	1.85	25.6	22.3	0.90
Schering	H Quality	Buy	1.58	1.76	1.83	19.7	18.9	0.69
SICOR	H Risk	S Buy	0.29	0.62	0.76	23.6	19.2	0.83
Watson Pharm	Speculative	Buy	1.19	1.62	1.58	17.7	17.2	0.62
Composite			*1.00*	*1.04*	*1.19*	*23.5*	*20.5*	*0.83*

Exhibit 9-10
Analyst Recommendations and Market Indicators — Con't
Pharmaceuticals Industry

| | Earnings Per Share Growth | | | | Beta | | L.T. Liab. |
	Last 5 Years	Last Year	Current Year	Next 5 Years	Coefficient	ROE	% of Cap.
Allergan	24	20	20	20	0.6	29	56
American Home	na	20	15	14	0.66	nm	na
Andrx Corp	na	2	180	na	0.72	21	17
Bristol Meyers	18	-5	13	9	0.64	46	15
Forest Labs	17	52	21	25	0.8	20	na
Heska Corp	na	nm	nm	na	1.55	nm	10
IVAX Corp	7	17	na	na	0.83	36	28
Lilly	20	-3	17	13	0.53	55	33
Merck	17	0	11	6	0.66	49	na
Mylan Labs	RVW						
Pfizer	8	23	15	16	0.76	30	6
Schering	18	11	4	11	0.81	43	na
SICOR	na	114	23	24	0.71	13	23
Watson Pharm	21	36	-2	13	0.5	13	31
Composite	*14*	*8*	*15*	*11*	*0.66*	*41*	*18*

In the **healthcare facilities** industry, the analyst has very strong opinions on many of the stocks in this industry. There is one stock that excels. Tenet Healthcare looks like the best stock in the group. It is only one of two good quality stocks in the industry. It is rated as a strong buy by the analyst, is growing as fast as the industry, has very consistent earnings growth, sells at a lower than industry P/E ratio and is well capitalized. It also has a good ROE.

Two companies in the **pharmaceuticals industry** look like the best to consider: Allergan and Pfizer. Allergan is a good quality company, the analyst has a strong buy recommendation for Allergan. The company has grown at a 24 percent rate for the past five years, and is estimated to grow 20 percent both this year and next. Over the next five years the company is expected to grow at a 20 percent rate in an industry that is projected to grow at 11 percent. Allergan is selling at a 29.6 P/E ratio for current earnings, and 24.7 times next years earnings compared to the industry average of 23.5 this year and 20.5 next year. While the P/E ratio is a bit higher than the industry composite, the PEG ratio, which is the P/E to growth rate, is about 1.5 for Allergan versus over 2 for the industry. All of these factors together make Allergan look like a good investment. It is worth taking quick look at some additional numbers. Allergan has been slightly less volatile than the industry with a beta of .60 versus an industry composite of .66, they have a 29 percent return on equity, lower than the 41 percent for the industry and 56 percent of their capitalization is represented by long term debt compared to 18 percent for the industry. Allergan is growing faster, has a higher P/E ratio, but a lower PEG ratio. They have a lower return on equity and are more highly leveraged, which needs to be considered. By looking at the numbers, this is a very interesting company that should be included in the portfolio if a detailed reading of the analyst report on the company continues to make the company look as good as our selection process does.

Pfizer is a very high-quality company with an analyst strong buy recommendation. Pfizer is forecast to grow at a 16 percent rate for the next five years — faster than its last five years rate of 8 percent. Pfizer's P/E ratio is modestly higher than the industry at 25.6 compared to 23.5 for the industry. Their PEG ratio is 1.6, which is on the lower end of the stocks being considered and under the industry. Pfizer has a beta of .76 which is higher than the industry, but the industry beta is significantly below the market. Pfizer has a 30 percent ROE and has only six percent of their capitalization represented by long-term debt. This should be another strong consideration for the portfolio after reading the analyst report in detail.

While we have yet to complete the last step of the process, we can be quite certain that several of these companies in the consumer staples sector will be part of our portfolio. By using this process of screening the sectors, industries and companies, we have identified just a few companies that deserve in-depth research.

The final step in this process is to read the analyst's report carefully on all stocks under consideration. In addition, read the companies' annual reports to get a sense of their businesses and their stories. The process is a narrowing one, and now you have to make your decisions.

Problems Using Research Sources
To show how problems can arise in using research, we

return to Exhibit 9-1 and the strategist's recommendations to place 15 percent of the portfolio in technology stocks. The strategist recommends under-weighting technology relative to the S & P 500, but a full 15 percent of the portfolio should be invested in this sector if you are starting from scratch and are following the strategist's guidelines. The strategist indicates that the following industries are good candidates for investment. The corresponding GICS relative strength category is given as well.

Exhibit 9-11
Strategist vs. Relative Strength
Classifications

Strategist	Relative Strength
Computer Services	Computer Storage & Peripheral
	IT Consulting Services
Electronics/Conductors	Office Electronics
	Semiconductor Equipment
Server Hardware & Appliances	Networking Equipment
Telecommunications Equipment	Telecom Equipment
Telecommunications Long-Distance	Integrated Telecommunications
Telecommunications Wireless	Wireless Telecommunications

We need to check these sectors against relative strength. The information technology sector chart shows that it is currently under-performing the market. The trend, in place since the late 1990s, shows no sign of shifting. It is too early to tell from the data whether technology has bottomed-out. Completing the selection of stocks in this sector will require a lot of thinking about how we use research sources to find a good answer, since both the strategist and the market are showing negative sentiments. We summarize the relative strength and analyst reports for the recommended sectors.

Exhibit 9-12
Information Technology Sector

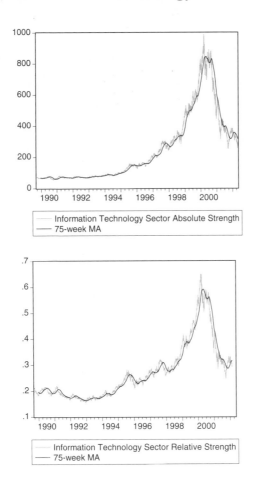

Exhibit 9-13
Computer Storage & Peripherals

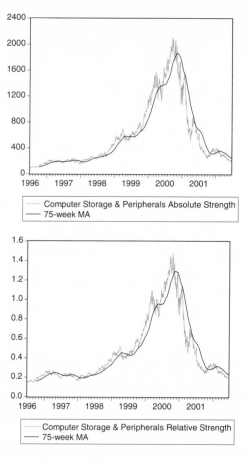

We can see from Exhibit 9-13 that this industry is on a downward trend. The analyst has half of the stocks in this industry under review, and the rest of the stocks have neutral ratings. The analyst rates one company as a speculative buy — Hewlett-Packard. Buying the only stock rated a buy in an industry is not a great investment move.

Exhibit 9-14
IT Consulting Services

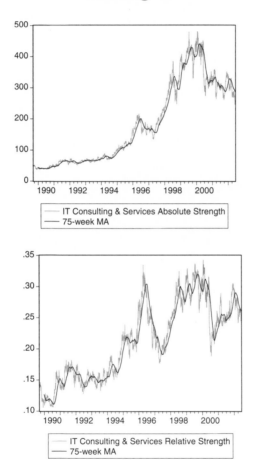

The **information technology services** industry is on an uptrend, but with a high degree of volatility. We will return to the specifics about the computer services industry at the end of this section.

Exhibit 9-15
Semiconductors Equipment

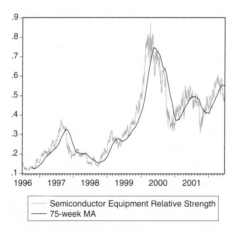

The **semiconductor equipment industry** looks like it may have bottomed-out. Of the 21 companies within the semiconductor equipment industry, nine have strong buy recommendations, and there are eight buys, three neutrals, and one sell recommendation.

Exhibit 9-16
Telecommunications Sector

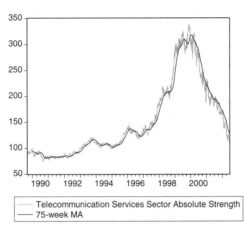

Telecommunication Services Sector Absolute Strength
75-week MA

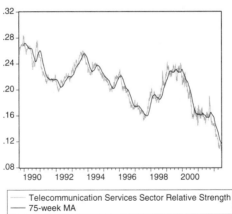

Telecommunication Services Sector Relative Strength
75-week MA

All of the **telecommunications industries**, like the overall sector, have strong downtrends in relative strength with no bottom in sight. The analyst reports for these industries are similarly neutral or negative.

Exhibit 9-17
Analyst Recommendations & Market Indicators
Computer Services

| Company | Quality | Opinion | Earnings Per Share | | | P/E Multiple | | P/E Relative |
			Last Year Actual	Current Year Est.	Next Year Est.	This Year	Next Year	to Market
Affiliated Corp	Spec	Strong Buy	2.46	3.51	4.20	26.7	22.3	0.94
Automatic Data	H Quality	Buy	1.59	1.75	2.00	30.9	27.0	1.09
BISYS Group	Spec	Strong Buy	1.47	1.93	2.29	32.4	27.3	1.14
Ceridian Corp	Spec	Buy	0.55	0.81	0.97	21.3	17.8	0.75
Convergys	Spec	Neutral	1.24	1.55	1.80	21.0	18.1	0.74
DST Systems	G Quality	Neutral	1.60	1.80	ne	23.7	na	0.83
EDS	Spec	Buy	2.68	3.35	ne	17.5	na	0.62
Exult	H Risk	Strong Buy	1.59d	0.03	ne	407.0	na	14.31
First Data	G Quality	Strong Buy	2.82	3.30	3.80	24.8	21.5	0.87
Fiserv	G Quality	Strong Buy	1.07	1.36	1.63	30.2	25.2	1.06
Paychecx Inc	G Quality	Neutral	0.68	0.73	0.84	48.5	42.1	1.70
Perot Systems	Spec	Buy	0.62	0.75	ne	23.8	na	0.84
Sungard Data	G Quality	Buy	0.82	0.87	1.13	35.8	27.6	1.26
Composite			*1.00*	*1.17*	*0.68*	*30.6*	*25.5*	*1.08*

Exhibit 9-17
Analyst Recommendations & Market Indicators – Con't
Computer Services

| | Earnings Per Share Growth | | | | Beta | | L.T. Liab. |
	Last 5 Years	Last Year	Current Year	Next 5 Years	Coefficient	ROE	% of Cap.
Affiliated Corp	27	43	20	20	0.73	17	27
Automatic Data	13	10	14	16	na	20	6
BISYS Group	33	31	19	20	0.65	19	34
Ceridian Corp	-2	47	20	12	0.86	9	39
Convergys	na	25	16	17	0.86	19	2
DST Systems	44	13	na	18	0.78	17	28
EDS	5	25	na	15	0.77	24	42
Exult	na	17	15	16	2.13	nm	na
First Data	na	17	15	16	1.01	24	30
Fiserv	na	27	20	19	0.82	15	15
Paychecx Inc	35	7	15	18	0.81	39	1
Perot Systems	na	21	15	na	0.34	12	na
Sungard Data	21	6	30	20	0.66	16	na
Composite	*19*	*15*	*18*	*17*	*0.92*	*27*	*21*

To summarize, the computer services industry and specifically the IT consulting industry looks fairly strong. The semiconductor equipment industry appears to be recovering. The telecommunications and the computer hardware industries look very weak at this time.

Within the analyst's report on computer services, he has four strong buy recommendations, nine buy recommendations and three neutral recommendations. We have the strategist, relative strength and the analyst all favoring the IT consulting/computer services industry. Exhibit 9-17 summarizes the specifics.

Using our analyst's recommendations and growth and valuation screens, the analyst's numbers suggest the following companies.

Affiliated Corp
Automatic Data
BISYS Group
First Data Corp
Fiserv

Automatic Data is not growing quite as fast as the industry, but it is the only high-quality stock, and it has a very good record. Affiliated Corp is a speculative company but has a strong buy rating, above industry growth and a better valuation than the industry. All of the five companies listed above have strong numbers and relative valuations and are worth exploring to find the best one or two for the technology portion of our portfolio. We recommend buying the highest-quality stock you can buy within an industry, subject to the company passing other screens. Use caution when purchasing these stocks and dollar-cost average into them over time.

The need to round out the portfolio motivates us to look at the electronics/conductors industry favored by the strategist and relative strength. Exhibit 9-18 summarizes the quality ratings, and Exhibit 9-19 gives the specifics on the highest-quality stock of the semi-conductor equipment industry.

Exhibit 9-18
Analyst Recommendations
Electronics Semiconductor Capital Equipment

Company	Quality	Rating
Advanced Energy	D High Risk	buy
Amkor Technology	D High Risk	buy
Applied Material	C Speculative	strong buy
Asyst	D High Risk	strong buy
ATMI Inc.	D High Risk	buy
Chippac Inc	D High Risk	strong buy
Cymer Inc.	D High Risk	neutral
Electro Sci	D High Risk	buy
EMCORE	D High Risk	strong buy
Entegris Inc	D High Risk	strong buy
KLA-Tencor	D High Risk	strong buy
Kulicke & Soffa	D High Risk	neutral
Lam Research	D High Risk	strong buy
MEMC Electronic	D High Risk	sell
MKS Instruments	D High Risk	strong buy
Novellus	D High Risk	strong buy
Photronics	D High Risk	buy
PRI Automaton	D High Risk	neutral
Silicon Valley	RVW	
Teradyne	D High Risk	buy
Ultratech	D High Risk	buy
Veeco Instr.	D High Risk	buy

Exhibit 9-19
Applied Material Market Indicators

Earnings

Last Year Actual	Current Year Est.	Next Year Est.	P/E Multiple		P/E Relative to Market
			This Year	Next Year	
2.39	1.03	0.19	39.6	214.7	1.28

Earnings Per Share Growth

Last 5 Years	Last Year	Current Year	Next 5 Years	Beta Coefficient	ROE	L.T. Liab. %of Cap.
32	n/a	-57	-82	1.9	36	7

Notice that the analyst rates all of the companies as high risk except for Applied Materials which he rates speculative. The analyst has nine strong buy recommendations, eight buy recommendations and only four neutral recommendations. Given the strategist's favorable recommendation on the office electronics industry and the favorable relative strength, Applied Materials, according to our initial screens, could provide some diversification within our group of information technology sector stocks. If you look closely at Exhibit 9-15, you will see the problem. Applied Materials has had a very erratic earnings history and has been very volatile. This is not a high-quality stock at this time. It looks like a pass for our conservative growth portfolio. This stock might be one to consider if you had a high-risk portfolio style and objective.

In summary, we will fill out our portfolio by dollar-cost averaging into IT consulting services stocks. While this position is concentrated, we have few choices if we stick to our discipline. It is likely that the strategist is early on some of his recommendations.

Troubleshooting

As a rule of thumb, if only two of the three research sources support investing in an industry, avoid the industry unless by doing so you move dramatically away from your benchmark. If risk management dictates, carefully purchase stocks in the less favored industries by dollar-cost-averaging over time. Choose only the best stocks from the less favored industries, so carefully analyze the fundamentals.

When only one of the research sources favors an

industry, invest only if you must for risk management and benchmark tracking purposes. If the strategist under-weights a sector, identify the industries he favors within the sector. Check those industries against relative strength and analyst reports. Use fundamentals to identify only the best stocks within those industries that have positive support from the market and the analyst. Dollar cost average into those stocks over time in order to round out the portfolio.

Because the strategist is sometimes early, we can focus research on the industries the strategist is recommending, even if the market is not currently favoring the industries. In this manner we learn more about the industries and companies within those industries. If we follow the relative strength charts on those recommended industries, we will be prepared to make good decisions once they begin to turn in favor of the industries

Completing Your Portfolio

To complete constructing the portfolio, proceed in the same manner with other recommended sectors through relative strength charts and analyst's reports to identify industries of interest. After you have identified the industries that you want to consider, examine the analyst reports for specific indicators such as quality and PEG ratios in order to identify companies that merit a further look. You should have a list of stocks to consider in detail at that point. When you have a list of stocks from the analyst's recommendations, do detailed research on the companies of interest. Read their annual reports, and read the specifics of the analyst's report on the company.

Where to Find Research Information

There is so much research information available from a broad variety of sources that the clutter associated with it all is a severe problem in itself. There are just a few sources of information that are comprehensive enough to provide an overall framework in which to work. Non-comprehensive sources should be used as secondary sources.

1. For comprehensive strategist research, look to the major full service brokerage firms. They are the best source. Many smaller firms purchase research from the larger firms, and therefore can not only provide you with the major research firms research, but also provide you with their own research to augment their total offering. There are several independent quality sources, but these sources frequently focus upon the institutional market, and their services are prohibitively priced for individuals and most financial advisors. Some services such as Value Line provide a fairly comprehensive amount of information, and are much more consistent than some of the major brokerage houses. This is an excellent source of comprehensive long-term historical data.

2. Industry analyst research is available from many sources. Many regional or smaller securities firms have focused company research that is excellent and not available from the major firms. There are also some Web sources that are useful. The problem with these sources as a primary source is that they are quite narrow in the number of companies they follow, and drop and add compa-

nies that are out or in favor. One will seldom see negative opinions from these sources unless that is their primary offering. Again, Value Line and other similar companies can be excellent sources for comprehensive information on industries.

3. Finding relative strength information is probably the most difficult part of the research puzzle. At least one of the major brokerage houses has excellent information. However, it has very inconsistent classifications for industries compared with the rest of the firm's research, and it is not widely used. Brokers who have access to the electronic Bridge System can use it to create relative strength charts, but this is time-consuming. Because of the lack of sources for relative strength charts, we have purchased the basic data from Standard & Poor's and publish this information on our Web site (*www.quantumrelativestrength.com*). At this time the service is free of charge.

4. Once individual stocks are selected for consideration, more in-depth research is required. The first step is to really "get to know" the company and its competitors. Good basic sources are Standard & Poor's stock reports, generally available from a financial advisor, and Value Line reports. Get your research reports from your primary source of research. Use the Internet to gather additional information. You can frequently go to the company's Web site, and there are many sources where you can find opinions and reports. Read these thoroughly, and then you will be ready to make your individual stock selections.

Instant X-ray on Morningstar is the best tool currently available to manage the sector, value-growth, and company size of portfolios. Input your portfolio and let Instant X-Ray analyze the portfolio details for you. You may have a portfolio that ends up too heavily weighted toward growth, based upon your objectives. Taking a little time, Morningstar provides a good way to assess where your entire portfolio, both individual stocks and mutual finds are, relative to the market and your goals each month.

Conclusion

In this chapter we discussed many research sources, and provided an example of how to construct a portion of a portfolio by using securities research in a systematic manner. We put the tools discussed in this book into practice, and have provided a comprehensive methodology for investing. If used, this approach will control and manage risk, and will likely increase long-term returns. Because our approach includes the use of research across several sources, implementing it involves both art and science. Putting it all together may be tricky at times, but the results will be a well diversified portfolio that yields good results.

An individual investor can follow the steps discussed in this chapter, but considering how serious the decisions are, the investor should probably find a partner. Like most things in life, partners are useful. We teach scouts the "buddy system" at the tender age of seven, and the basic premise applies throughout life — you are safer with a partner. In the case of investing, an experienced financial advisor can really help by providing comprehensive research and advice about constructing financial portfolios. Find a broker who has access to the major elements of research discussed in this book, and one with whom you agree on a set of disciplines. Our methodology also helps the partnership of investor and financial advisor work more smoothly by helping to establish rules for buying and selling stocks. We promise that communication between investor and financial advisor will be improved if the methods discussed here are implemented.

CHAPTER 10

Following Your Portfolio Over Time

How Market Dynamics Can Affect How You
Manage Your Portfolio

Once you have decided on a portfolio style, completed your research, and made decisions regarding the sectors, industries and stocks you want to emphasize, the question arises "How do I implement these ideas over time?" Some of the most common concerns investors have include the time they will have to spend managing the portfolio, whether to go it alone or find a financial advisor, how to time the purchases and sales of assets, and the tax consequences associated with buying and selling stocks. In this chapter, we address these issues and suggest concrete strategies for managing portfolios over time.

How Much Time Will I Have to Spend Researching and Managing my Stock Portfolio?

Investment Survival

If you choose to manage your own investments, you should undertake a monthly assessment of your portfolio. Once you have constructed a good portfolio, put methods in place to monitor and make adjustments to the portfolio over time. The good news is that by using the approach we have presented in Chapters 5 through 9, the amount of time you need to stay current is only a couple of hours a month and difficult decisions are made more easily. By using the specified screening process we have described, it is easy to sort through the barrage of articles, data, advertising and recommendations available. Once you know what is important to your investment process, all you need to do is to find information sources, organize them, and do your research on a regular basis. The following should help you organize your research.

First, major market trends adjust slowly. Review the strategists' recommendations once a month to stay current. Look to see if there are any meaningful changes. Unless there is a major shock (that by definition is unpredictable), a strategist will not change his recommendations quickly. Strategists may tweak their recommended portfolio weights a bit, but major changes such as going from under-weighting to over-weighting occur over months or even years. Financial advisors typically notify their clients about any major revisions. Our experience has been that watching strategists for changes in their recommendations is a slower process than watching paint dry! Remember that strategists make their recommended changes early, giving the analysts and portfolio managers time to do their homework before they need to make changes in their investment positions.

Second, a monthly review of relative strength data

keeps you current. Use relative strength to confirm the strategists' recommendations and to access timely information regarding when to implement strategists' changes. The trends in relative strength seldom change in less than 18 months to two years, and in some cases last up to 10 years. Your review for the most part will indicate that there are few significant changes. When changes do begin to occur, they will be evident and should catch your attention. Watch to see if the observed changes are simple market blips, or if they indicate real change. When you recognize a blip, begin asking questions and do research with other sources to see if anything meaningful is happening.

Third, examine the analyst reports. Look for changes in opinions. Most of the major sources of research publish a list of opinion upgrades, downgrades and new companies covered, but they are not terribly accommodating on listing the companies that are dropped from coverage. If coverage on a company is dropped, this is a red flag to signal you to go to work and research in order to find out why. Analysts may drop companies for a number of reasons, including:

1. The analyst covering the industry has left the firm and the firm has not replaced him.
2. A firm has hired a new or replacement analyst. The new analyst might have a different perspective on the companies in the industry.
3. Some firms' research departments drop all coverage on the companies in an industry if they do not find that the industry is favorable in the market. They focus their limited analyst staff on the parts

of the market that they see as positive and ignore the rest. When a firm drops coverage, it leaves the investor in a very uncomfortable situation.

4. Another possible reason why a company is dropped is that the analyst is simply covering fewer firms within an industry. For these and many other reasons we believe it is prudent to have at least two sources of analyst opinions.

In all of these cases, you should consider downgrading your holdings of the dropped company, either because you can't follow it, or because the analyst doesn't perceive it as being that significant in the industry, unless you can find another quality source of research. If you don't have an analyst's opinion on your holdings, you must actively manage the situation. You are on your own, and that is a risky place to be. You no longer have support from the analyst on whose research you based your purchases.

Sometimes analysts following an industry will place all of the companies in an entire industry under review. The analyst may not have a problem with the industry, but is dropping coverage of the industry to focus on other parts of the market. The review signals that the analyst is not paying much attention to the industry at the time. Another possibility is that the analyst has questions about the industry that need further probing. In either case, you don't have information on the industry at your disposal, and this is not a good thing. Clarify the reasons for the change in coverage. If you can't find an answer, which will most likely be the case, try to find an alternative source for information. If no other source is available, move the money in this investment to an industry in which you do have confidence and research support.

Fourth, examine changes in earnings estimates. One of the disciplines we have found helpful is to watch for two changes in earnings estimates in the same direction, either up or down. The second change acts as a confirmation that the first change was not a blip. Two earnings estimate decreases indicate that you take a very hard look at the stock, and that you need a really good reason not to sell it. Make sure that the change is because of a real difference in what the company is doing and not just an analyst "tweaking" the earnings estimate by one or two cents. Sometimes analysts will tweak their estimates when outside groups rate them on the accuracy of their projected earnings.

It is better to sell the stock when it is questionable. A useful question to ask is whether you would buy the stock under current circumstances if you did not already own it. You can always buy it back after taking a fresh objective review of the company. Taking a good look at the firm will likely convince you that your money is better invested elsewhere for the time being. If you want to buy it back in the future, a round turn in commissions is a very small price to pay for the insurance of having an objective new look at the company. Several years ago, one bank trust investment officer we know employed a practice of forcing a sale in tax-exempt accounts whenever any bad news occurred, or after the investor had held a stock for 24 months. Portfolio managers sold the stock under this directive, but could buy it back immediately if they thought it was the best place to put the money. Reinvestment in the same stock rarely happened, and the accounts managed in this manner performed very well.

What is true for the company is also true of the industry. Examine opinions on earnings estimates across several companies within any industry. Overall changes for the industry will be reflected in changes in earnings estimates. Take a deeper look at industries where the balance of the opinions changed, in either the positive or negative direction. Review all your research sources to either reaffirm your previous decisions or make adjustments.

Periodic reviews are important. Most of the time, you will have to make relatively few adjustments. When indicated, you are much better informed to make good choices regarding portfolio adjustments. Review the sector allocation of your stock portfolio on a monthly to quarterly basis. On a quarterly to semi-annual basis, review the overall asset allocation portfolio weights to see how they changed with market movements. Re-allocate funds to return your portfolio to the mix you chose as a matter of policy. Re-assess your asset allocation policy with major life changes, not with market movements. When anything triggers a deeper look, immediately check each step we have outlined to see if there is any confirmation of the information that caused the alert. Lacking a confirmation should not be a comfort. Proceed to dig deeper into the specific company. Understand the reason for the red flag. Beyond the monthly review, twice a year you should walk through your entire process to reaffirm your holdings.

Use the process in this book, or develop one of your own. A good process should bring all of the fragmented market information together systematically as part of a comprehensive building and monitoring system. Judge any approach you adopt on its ease of use and time efficiency, because if an approach takes too long, you will be less likely to follow it regularly. There will be times when any process works. There will be times when no process works. But, having an inconsistent approach to the market rarely works.

Going it Alone or Finding a Partner?

A partner, who is a highly-qualified professional financial advisor, can be invaluable when implementing this process for managing an investment portfolio. Working with a professional partner will dramatically decrease the investor's workload with the added benefit that the partner is a full-time professional. A good financial advisor will undertake most of the research for you, and will provide you with summary reports of opinions and earnings estimates as well as analyst changes of earnings estimates and opinions for your review. If there is a major change in trend, the professional financial advisor will immediately inform you. Trained financial advisors are better able to interpret and stay abreast of market trends than the average investor, in the same way physicians are better able to prescribe appropriate medications than are their patients. Clients working with professional financial advisors, according to Gomez Research, only do half as many transactions as do investors working alone on the Internet. One of the most productive things that financial advisors do is they talk investors out of making bad decisions.

A financial advisor can be very valuable in implementing this process. Consider these guidelines when choosing a financial advisor/broker:

Tips on Finding a Good Financial Advisor/Broker:
1. Hands-on experience counts for a lot. Proven results and reasonable success over a significant time period is the single most significant criteria for expertise, regardless of formal education or designations.
2. Don't look for a financial advisor until you think about what you want the advisor to do for you. Be clear about your wishes. Write them down to take with you when you interview candidates. Ask yourself, do you want to lead in the investment process, or do you want to follow? Do you want to be actively involved in the research, or do you want the advisor to do it for you, providing brief summaries only? Do you want an aggressive growth account, or are you looking for a core management style? Brokers cannot professionally provide unique services to each client. Don't try to get a broker to do something that they do not normally do!
3. Ask people you trust, who they use as financial advisors. Make sure that the people you ask have significant stock portfolios of their own. Ask them about their investment philosophies. When their philosophies sound similar to your own, ask for the name and number of their financial advisors and set up interviews.
4. Interview more than one advisor. You want to find an advisor who specializes in the kinds of services you desire. Good advisors will be seeking clients who want and need what they have to offer. Different financial advisors have different

skill sets. Ask about their clients. Are they like you? Weed out any brokers whose clients are substantially different from you in terms of income, social position, profession etc. You don't want to be the broker's smallest account. Weed out brokers who have too huge of a client list. You don't want to work with someone who has no time for you. Many brokers have so many accounts that they either ignore some accounts altogether or they do not have enough time to provide even minimal services for their clients. If a financial advisor has over 2000 client relationships, his time is too scarce to serve individual clients well. There are 2000 working hours in a year. If you divide the number of accounts an advisor has into that number, you will clearly see how much time they will have to spend with you!

5. Consider the advisors on your short list. Do you like them? Only choose to work with an advisor with whom you have good chemistry. Otherwise, the relationship will be too much of a burden for both of you. Ask the broker to tell you his story. Is it compelling? Consider whether the advisor is the type of person you would be willing to help professionally (or personally), if he asked.

6. Before settling on a financial advisor, inquire about his or her training. Within the industry there was much focus on marketing, gathering assets and selling managed or packaged products. If you have an inadequately trained financial advisor on your list, remove him. You might be asking, "How can I tell if the advisor is well

trained?" The following points will help:

a. Does the advisor have a CFP? CFP is a Certified Financial Planner. This designation involves a very detailed and rigorous education, but includes very little investment training.

b. Does the advisor have a CFA? CFA is a Chartered Financial Analyst. The CFA is an extremely difficult program and is almost exclusively focused on investing. It takes a minimum of three years to receive this certification beyond formal college education. CFAs typically work as professional analysts or portfolio managers. If you find a broker who is also a CFA, it is highly unusual and a very good thing.

c. Does the advisor have a CLU? CLU is a Chartered Life Underwriter. This person will have most of his training in insurance and estate planning.

d. Does the advisor have a CFM? CFM is a unique designation available to Merrill Lynch brokers that involves comprehensive investment, planning, marketing and client service training. The advisor will have received some advanced investment training, but it is not nearly as extensive as the training involved in obtaining a CFA.

e. Does the advisor have a ChFC? ChFC is a Chartered Financial Consultant. They focus on insurance and financial planning for individuals. They often are highly skilled in insurance related financial assets, such as annuities, but the designation requires little formal investment training.

f. Does the advisor have a PFS? A PFS is a Personal Financial Specialist which is a designation exclusively for CPAs who are members of the American Institute of CPAs. They have skill on a wide range of personal financial matters, focusing on tax related concerns.

g. Does the advisor have a CIC? A CIC is a Chartered Investment Counselor. The CIC is an additional designation beyond the CFA, and requires candidates to demonstrate significant expertise in performing investment counseling and portfolio management responsibilities. The designation that the holder be employed by an Investment Counsel Association of America (ICAA) member firm, have significant work and character references and endorse the ICAAs Standards of Practice.

h. There are many other types of designations and certifications. If you are interviewing someone and she mentions a designation that you do not know, simply ask her to explain it in detail.

i. Most of the outstanding financial advisors we have known are long on experience and highly educated, but have few of the formal designations. Without extensive experience, the designations become more important.

7. Ask your candidates what type of investment research they use. Do they use their firm's resources that are available to them? What outside resources of information do they rely upon?

Do they have an organized method for implementing their use? Make sure that the advisor is portfolio oriented, and not simply a good stock picker.

8. Ask to look at some portfolios of clients that are currently working with the advisor. Advisors are naturally reluctant to break confidentiality. If they provide the information, check to see that they maintained the privacy of the account holder, unless you don't mind your portfolio being shown to others. Just make sure that you and the advisor have the same philosophy regarding confidentiality.

After you have gone through these steps, you should have a very short list of candidates. Choose the one who you have the best gut feeling about. Trust your instincts.

Strategies for Success

Whether you work alone or with a partner, you may want to simplify and at the same time diversify your portfolio using a *core portfolio strategy*. With this approach, the investor buys the benchmark for the portfolio in the form of an index fund. For example, purchase 70 to 80 percent of the portfolio in an S & P 500 index fund. With the other 20 to 30 percent, focus on specific higher risk, higher potential investments. If your portfolio is in a tax-deferred account, there are no tax implications with this approach. If your portfolio is taxable, the capital gains and losses realized by the fund are subject to tax, as the fund adds and drops stocks from its holdings. "Large cap" index funds will often have capital losses, because the companies dropped are usually dropped because of poor performance, mergers, spin-offs, or acquisitions. "Mid cap" and "small cap" indices include companies that are dropped for the same reasons as "large caps" drop companies, but they also sell shares of companies that have done well but have grown in their capitalization category. For example, Microsoft and Cisco could have moved from "small cap" to "mid cap" to "large cap" classifications, generating capital gains within index funds and associated tax obligations to the investors.

Another approach is to use an investment manager who uses a core style of management. Individual stock core portfolio managers should provide value by either performing better than the benchmark or provide less risk than the benchmark. One place index funds will not work is when an investor's portfolio has a very large exposure to a single stock or industry. If the investor holds the large position separate from the managed portfolio, the core portfolio manager can exclude the outside exposure to a specific stock or industry — an index cannot.

If you desire "higher octane" in your portfolio, use the 20 to 30 percent of the portfolio to invest in individual stocks where you and your advisor have expert knowledge. Another strategy is to purchase specialized funds, such as sector, industry or leveraged funds, focusing upon the sectors forecasted to out-perform the index.

We often hear the question "When building and managing my portfolio, how do I choose the optimal time to buy and sell?" The best answer to the question is "Don't try to find the optimal time!" Performance measurement of professional managers shows that almost no one adds value by timing the market over the period of three years or more. You can neutralize the impact of where the market is, and its affect on your portfolio when buying or selling stocks, with a buying strategy known as *dollar cost averaging*. By using the strategy, you avoid large financial decisions such as creating a whole new investment portfolio with a large amount of money.

One of the benefits from dollar cost averaging is that by doing it this way, you avoid market timing. All investors face the question about whether it is the right time to invest. Investors often avoid adding to securities investments because they perceive the market to be over-valued or turbulent. It is impossible to identify the perfect day for investing, except by looking at history, and then you have missed the opportunity. Rather than be paralyzed by trying to find the perfect time to invest a large amount of money, invest smaller amounts periodically to reach the longer-term goal. In this way you spread the implementation over a longer period of time by systematically making incremental decisions and changes.

Using a dollar cost averaging approach, you invest the same amount of money regularly in a specific investment, like a mutual fund or stock portfolio, paying the going price at the time the money is invested. Your portfolio will grow most effectively if you add to it regularly. If you commit to investing at least once a month or quarter, you create the portfolio and level out risk over a selected time period. This strategy eliminates worries about the best time to invest. Ideally, you want to buy low and sell high, but waiting for the best time to buy can be paralyzing and costly.

Following Your Portfolio Over Time

It bears repeating previous comments about playing the market timing game. The stock market stayed in a channel under 1000 in the Dow Jones industrial average from 1965 through 1980. Investors and technicians became convinced that getting in and out of the market was one of the keys to investing success. As the market began to rise in the 1980s, many well know technical analysts advised caution. They recommended holding money on the sidelines, and waiting for market corrections. When the Dow reached 2700, and then 3500, they cautioned investors again. The models that were indicating caution were based upon the past. What had worked relatively well during the 1970s was a disaster during the 1980s and 1990s. When markets continued rising investors who held cash and waited lost opportunities that they would never recapture. Staying fully invested can be very difficult, but by being well positioned when the market recovers allows recapture and upswing. Choosing the best sectors and industries for the recovery should be the focus of research efforts.

Dollar cost averaging is one of the oldest strategies on Wall Street. This strategy allows you to buy more stock when the market prices are low and less stock when the market prices are high. Since the share price of every stock or fund moves up and down as the market changes, adding a fixed dollar amount to your portfolio at regular intervals will sometimes yield more stock and sometimes less stock. The more expensive the price per share, the fewer shares you can afford, and vice versa. As you purchase stock at a high price and at a low price, your average cost per share may end up lower than the average share price as the text box example shows.

Dollar Cost Averaging Example

	May	**June**	**July**	**August**
Amount invested	$100	$100	$100	$100
Average share price per month	$22	$17	$14	$18
Number of shares purchased	4.55	5.88	7.14	5.56

Average Share Price = Average price per months/ Number of months

($22 + $17 + $14 + $18)/4 = $17.75

Average Share Cost = Total amount invested/Total shares purchased

$400/ (4.55 + 5.88 + 7.14 + 5.56) = $17.29[1]

If you are constructing a stock portfolio from scratch, apply the principle of dollar cost averaging to the accumulation of stock after you have gone through all the steps to identify good stocks for your portfolio (see Chapter 9 for the steps). If you are rebalancing a portfolio, accumulate new purchases by dollar cost averaging. If you are selling stock to reduce a large position, apply the same principles in reverse.

Tax and Other Deterrents to Diversification

In our discussions with investors, we often hear their concerns about the tax consequences of adjusting their stock portfolios. Diversifying a portfolio often leads to taxable capital gains. During bull markets this problem is especially severe since investors don't have capital losses to offset the gains. After-tax returns are the ultimate goal. An investor should avoid taxes that can be avoided and defer taxes that can be deferred. A policy of keeping winners and selling losers often makes a lot of sense. The obvious exception is when the winners become too large as to disrupt portfolio diversification.

There are several other common situations that lead investors to avoid portfolio diversification because of tax considerations. One involves a portfolio with one or two very large positions of securities with very low-cost tax basis. These highly-concentrated portfolios are often the result of stock ownership from employment relationships, such as stock options or deferred stock grants that were restricted for a period of time. Another common problem is a concentrated stock position from the sale of a private company in exchange for stock in a tax-free exchange. In many cases, the stocks in question represent quality companies that have appreciated at an above- market rate and still have very promising outlooks. A third common situation is when stock is inherited. Investors are often reluctant to sell shares in stock that have contributed to their wealth, or they may have emotional connections to the company because of the predecessor. Some people feel that they are betraying the giver's legacy if they sell the stock they were given. In all of these cases, the investor faces the dilemma of realizing the capital gains versus maintaining the excess risk with lack of diversification.

In order to make reasonable decisions about managing a portfolio, assess the risk of maintaining such a large position. If you have large positions in minor sectors of the market (for example, sectors representing only three percent of the market), extremely over-weighting your portfolio in those sectors would be a problem because you are so far removed from the benchmark. Undertaking a portfolio review helps the investor to quantify risk, and then more easily identify the amount of stock that might be sold to bring the portfolio into balance and closer to the benchmark.

Some of the most severe cases of lost wealth from holding extremely large positions in a single stock occur when people own large percentages of a company's stock in the form of founder's stock. During the years just before and after the turn of the 21st century, many people went from major wealth to bankruptcy. Some investors had all their wealth in one stock, and then borrowed against the stock when it was at a high level. The combination of the fall in stock price and the debt obligation was very, very costly.

Once the size of the portfolio imbalance is determined, the issue can be framed in terms of the investor's overall financial situation. If the concentrated stock position is 20 percent of the owner's total net worth, or is less than a few years of the owner's annual income (assuming that he is planning to continue working), the large position is not life threatening. It is just risky. On the other hand, if the investor holds 80 percent of his total net worth in one stock, or his annual income is small relative to the holdings, the risk to the investor's well-being is great. In the second case, diversification should be a priority in order to achieve a safe investment posture.

Tax considerations are one of the biggest reasons why people don't diversify. In some cases, the cost basis of the stock is near zero and the investor would have to pay tax, probably long-term, on almost all of the value. Investors understand that holding an appreciated stock allows the deferral of taxes owed to the government. In essence, the have an interest-free loan, and the investor has the option about the timing of liquidating the position and paying the tax. On the other hand, the benefit of the interest-free loan is not great enough to outweigh the potential losses of an overly-concentrated portfolio. The maximum tax rate on long-term gains is 20 percent federally, plus a bit more where states have income taxes on long-term gains. The late 1990s showed that losing 20 percent or more of one's capital is quite possible. Looking back, many people would now have rather paid the tax bill! One only needs to consider almost every dot.com company and many technology companies at the turn of the 21st century. Companies such as Xerox, Kodak, Syntex and Enron all had the same experience. Many investors held large positions in these companies thinking that the tax consequences were too great, and the companies were too good. Don't avoid paying the 20 percent, given the potential losses. When significant wealth is achieved, preservation of that wealth must be a primary consideration. One can look back, regretting the sale of a stock that only appreciated after the sale, but the benefits of risk reduction are profound.

Conclusion

Managing a stock portfolio over time is a challenging process. You may choose to do it alone, but we suggest you find a good partner. The issues are complicated, and often involve making decisions under stress. A financial advisor/partner can talk you out of making big mistakes. You and your partner need a process, and strategies for implementing it. Use the research, follow the dollar cost averaging approach to growing and rebalancing the portfolio and be wise about taxes.

CHAPTER 11

Global and Zero Correlation
Investments

Hedge Funds, International Investing and Other
Ways to Add "Octane" to Your Portfolio

T he financial industry is evolving rapidly. Innovation doesn't only happen in the laboratory. Financial assets are being packaged in new and excit-
ing ways. Some strategies hedge against one type of
risk, while simultaneously ramping up the risk in another
area in order to increase returns. Management strategies
that were once only available to a few ultra-wealthy individuals and the institutional market are becoming widely
available to the investing public. The democratization of
Wall Street is continuing. As with any democracy, education is vital. The new products make it only more criti-
cal that the investor educate himself and/or work with a
financial advisor as a partner who makes it a priority to

educate himself and educate his clients.

This chapter discusses more advanced investing strategies and questions, but does not provide detailed research advice about these topics. The securities research discussed in the earlier chapters of this book focuses primarily on listed and NASD stocks. In some cases, that research will still be useful in addressing advanced topics, as with global investing. In other cases, that research falls short, as with hedge funds. We intend this chapter as a guide to begin the process of becoming more educated about newer products and services. If you have learned the lessons in this book, you'll be thinking about how to construct a process for organizing information about the advanced strategies. Even if you totally rely on the advice from your financial advisor, it pays to educate yourself, and to use research to review your accounts on a monthly basis.

We have made a case for taking a long-term approach to investing in the stock market, and introduced a process to add alpha to your diversified portfolio of stocks. Beyond the asset allocation decision discussed in Chapter 2, we have avoided discussion of the bond and money markets. In this chapter, we discuss some bond and money market derivatives. It might seem counter intuitive to discuss these assets, while making an argument for the stock market, but some derivatives provide risk/return profiles very similar to the stock market and are used by some investors as equity substitutes. We are not advocating any of these approaches to investing. Our goal is to provide information about alternatives available to enhance performance.

Global Investing: Should I Invest Globally?

Global investing is an advanced topic for several reasons. The first is that information about international companies and international politics has not been as easy to access for American investors. Secondly, changes in exchange rates complicate the decision process, since there is an extra source of volatility and potential return. The third is that there are many questions about the behavior of international stocks over the last 20 years that are not easily answered. Let us explain.

During the later part of the 20th century, foreign and emerging market investing provided outstanding returns. The United States market grew more slowly than many foreign economies, providing incentive to invest in the rapid growth of other countries and newer markets. Economists and modern portfolio practitioners argued that by adding international investments to a portfolio, the portfolio would be less volatile (safer) and have higher total returns. Investors were searching for the "efficient frontier" of risk/return optimization. Investors and brokers happily participated in these new opportunities. Products such as country funds, emerging market funds, international funds and global funds caught the imagination of the globally-oriented public.

The first inkling that the global approach might be more risky than previously understood involved the economic growth leader, Japan. The Japanese market performed phenomenally until the "bursting of the bubble economy." After the "bubble," the Japanese economy faltered and stagnated. Japanese financial markets tumbled. The Japanese stock index fell by almost 60 percent during the 1990s. As of 2002, economists still do not fully understand why the Japanese economy has stagnated for so long, or why the "bubble" burst when it did and with such severity. We do understand that the performance of the global index was severely affected by the Japanese market performance, because the "bubble" in Japanese stock prices bid up the market capitalization of those stocks within the index. Since the index was capitalization weighted, the overall performance of the index suffered as Japan suffered.[1]

As the Japanese economy faltered, other countries faced severe economic problems. Economists began to discover the severity of the Russian post-communist collapse of their fledgling new market economy and securities markets. Emerging markets struggled to maintain badly-needed capital, as the flight from risky capital to the safe haven of the United States occurred. The U.S. markets reaped major benefits from the safe haven effects and our relatively healthy economy during the 1990s. International investing lost much of its luster.

While many emerging markets have suffered severe declines, and some countries have serious current problems, many of these countries are beginning to recover and will grow much faster than the U.S. economy in the future. Over the long-term, international investing may indeed reward investors as markets recover, but major risks stand in the way of investor confidence. As of the writing of this book, most Latin American and Asian economies have not addressed the problems surrounding taxation, banking and monetary policy, increasing the risk of investing in that region. Russia is plagued by a lack of the basic rule of law. Japan's economy continues to be closed and over-regulated. Many Asian economies suffer unstable governments and corruption. The accounting practices throughout the world limit investors' access to good data about global companies. Western Europe seems to be the exception to the rule in terms of international investing, begging the question, "Should investors add global investments to their portfolios?"

The answer is "yes" for the long-term investor. One area of confusion to the investor is exactly how we define global investing. This term refers to investing in the most attractive sectors, industries and companies throughout the world, including U.S. markets. Global investing involves exposures to global risk. Investments in U.S. securities already involve a significant exposure to global risk, because business transactions take place in global markets. It is easy to understand why a multinational corporation would be exposed to global risks, since those corporations have offices worldwide and dealings in many nations. What is harder to understand is why a United States-based corporation that has no global sources or markets might be exposed to global risks. These risks stem from their competition. If the competition is a firm in another county, the U.S. firm is exposed to risks associated with the exchange rate, labor costs and government policies in the other country because these things affect the competitions' pricing. The United States has almost totally lost the market for television, small appliances and other consumer electronic products, first to Japan, and now to other Asian countries that have replaced Japan as primary suppliers of these products. Globalization has changed the risk profiles of domestic firms, and has blurred the line between the concepts of domestic and international.

Exchange rate exposure is an important variable for investors. For example, if a domestic firm makes and sells shoes solely in the United States it faces the risks of shoe imports from Italy. If the euro depreciates relative to the dollar, Italian shoes become cheaper, providing risk to the U.S. shoe company. Companies facing international competition often hedge against currency exposure by purchasing foreign exchange futures and forward contracts. Investors may want to hedge against currency exposure as well. Other investors may want to take active positions on currency exposure.

Investors can address global markets by either placing their money in professionally-managed global funds, or they can build a portfolio sensitive to global risks by including U.S. companies with a variety of global exposures, such as Coca-Cola. The percentage of the portfolio invested in global assets is a policy choice. Once that decision is made, one must decide how much foreign exchange exposure they want. The investor will need to hedge all of the exposure or a portion of it if they are investing directly in companies whose stock prices are quoted in foreign currency. Major U.S. companies that face significant foreign exchange exposure normally hedge. These issues are complicated, and a good portfolio manager or advisor can add significant value here.

Alternative Investments

There are many money management strategies other than investing solely in publicly-traded stocks. The most obvious of the alternative strategies would be to directly invest in a company that has yet to go public. Identifying excellent private companies that have potential to

232

grow rapidly with capital infusion is difficult for most investors. Beyond private investing, many strategies are created such that they are absolutely uncorrelated with the stock market. Some are used to enhance performance beyond the market return and others are used to level the volatility of the total return on the portfolio. The latter strategy is particularly important when the overall market performance is negative. Often these uncorrelated money management strategies are referred to as *zero correlation investments.* We will discuss these alternative investments in the section below.

Private Investing

Only very experienced and risk-oriented investors should participate in private investments. Investing in companies that are not publicly traded is a risky business, and it is one of the investment alternatives that is still closely correlated to the public stock markets. In many cases, private investing means investing in start-up companies, publicly-traded companies that are going private, companies in bankruptcy, or company spin-off's. With private investing you take on liquidity risk in addition to principal risk. Your main exit strategy is an "initial public offering" (IPO) that may or may not occur. An investor may have to hold an investment for five to 10 years and longer, and have no way to liquidate if the company has problems or begins to fail.

This type of investing was very successful during the 1980s and 1990s, but it is unclear whether the market for initial public offerings will be as profitable over the next 20 years. Recall that style preferences change with time, and the success of this type of investing is highly dependent upon the overall state of the economy. A healthy stock market and good set of institutional structures are vital to the success of private investing.

Sometimes private investing involves the purchase of an interest in a venture or private investment fund rather than making direct investments. Companies that manage private investments or venture funds are usually paid a fee as a percentage of assets, plus a percentage of the profits. They oversee the company, make additional investments to keep a company going, sit on the board of directors and provide expertise and management advice. If necessary, they replace management or close the company. The historical return on well-managed private investment funds is outstanding. Some investments have been a disaster, but on balance the return has been above the market.

Investors who participate in these funds typically invest in several in order to spread risk. In most cases investors must be "accredited investors," and purchase an interest in the fund. "Accredited investors" have significant wealth, high incomes, and investment experience. Regulations are in place requiring that the investor understand the risks and the low liquidity of the investments. The investor must have enough resources in his overall portfolio to handle the risks.

Many private investment funds are taking the "fund of funds" approach. The fund of funds approach is a multi-manager portfolio of private investments that the investor can access through one fund of funds. This approach helps investors qualify and diversify their investments. Managers select different private or venture funds, based on their forecasts of economic growth and the particulars of the funds themselves. It is quite possible that these "fund of funds" will invest in companies that will become great public stocks of the future.

Hedge Funds

Hedge funds provide a different approach to investing. Rather than seeking excess returns relative to a benchmark, hedge funds seek high risk-adjusted absolute returns. The typical hedge fund invests both long and short in the stock market. The strategy is designed to be uncorrelated with the market itself. The hedge fund manager seeks positive returns, regardless of the overall market direction. Hedge funds exploit market inefficiencies such as irregular bid/ask spreads, liquidity changes and market trends, and are thus deemed arbitrage strategies. An alternative use of the term hedge fund describes financial strategies that involve high degrees of leverage. Leveraging involves borrowing in order to enhance returns. While leveraging and hedging are different, some leveraged strategies are referred to as hedge funds. In addition, many hedge funds offer leveraged strategies.

Hedge funds are not without risk, but are designed to meet specific risk mandates. The success of a hedge fund is highly dependent upon the skill of the individual manager, because the fund is designed to be uncorrelated with the overall market. There is no market beta in the portfolio. Bull markets don't affect hedge fund returns, because the portfolio is uncorrelated with the market. The manager's experience in identifying market inefficiencies leads to good performance. Because successful hedge funds are so linked to the skills of their managers, investors gain significantly by diversifying. Diversification is even more important with hedge funds than with portfolios that track a benchmark.

In order to better diversify, a number of "fund of fund" products are now available. The "fund of fund" selects hedge funds and allows the investor a smaller investment in each of several hedge funds. In order to invest in a hedge fund, you often must be an accredited investor, meeting risk tolerance, income and asset standards. Minimum investments in hedge funds are as low as $25,000, but most start at $250,000 or higher.

Because of the nature of the assets, hedge fund managers often place "locks" on investors of a year or more. Managers sometimes require that investors give advanced notice when they want to liquidate their assets of 30 to 90 days. On the other hand, the assets of the funds often grow beyond what the managers can effectively manage, given the strategies they employ. A capacity constraint is when an excessively large account limits the control the manager has over the strategies he is implementing. For example, in order to make a short sell, one has to borrow someone's stock to deliver when the stock is sold short. There are limits to the amount of stock that can be borrowed, thus the manager is limited to a maximum amount he can invest in this strategy. If a hedge fund faces capacity constraints, the manager might make major distributions to the investors. When assets within the fund become too large, the manager will close the fund and return some of the investment capital. Some hedge funds have made single distributions larger than the original investment.

Affluent individuals own 80 percent of hedge funds,

with the balance owned by pension funds, endowments and foundations. Institutions are currently providing most of the growth in this market (Newsweek, March 11, 2002).

Because of the high returns on hedge funds, the demand for their products is growing rapidly. With account size limits, new firms entering the market must meet the demand for this management style. The obvious question that arises from the growth of new firms is "Where do the hedge funds find qualified, skilled and experienced managers?" Manager skill creates the value in investment strategy. Many new funds simply do not have experienced managers. Caution is warranted.

Other High-Yielding Strategies

1. *Distressed Security Portfolio Strategy* — the manager purchases junk bond debt and equity in companies near bankruptcy that the manager expects to recover.
2. *Acquisitions Strategies* — some funds purchase stock in companies that are targeted to be acquired, while selling short those companies doing the acquiring.
3. *Convertible Arbitrage Funds* — these funds buy bonds that are convertible into common stock, and simultaneously sell the stock short, taking advantage of the spread.
4. *Leveraged Strategies* — these funds monitor the spreads on yields in different categories and maturities of bonds.
5. *Currency Funds* – This type of investing seeks out spreads in currencies.

The above strategies are just a few of the possible investments that are designed to be uncorrelated with the market benchmark. They are absolute returns strategies with associated risk profiles. The risk in each of these strategies can be increased or decreased with leveraging techniques. Decisions to invest in these strategies should weigh the forecasted absolute return of these strategies against the next best alternative. The success of alternative strategies is highly dependent upon the skill of the managers, so use caution. Further, each strategy has a unique set of tax consequences.

Conclusion

New financial management techniques and products evolve regularly. Management styles become popular and then some lose their luster. It is easy to be swept away by a wave of excitement over a process that is currently yielding very high returns, only to end up drowned in enormous losses.

If you invest in a hedge fund or high-risk strategy, understand the nature of the risk and diversify. The "fund of funds" approach provides a good way to do so. Be smart. Educate yourself. Avoid strategies that you don't understand well, and be wary of strategies that have had phenomenal past performance. Maintain your basic investment principles. If newer strategies work within your ideals and goals and you understand them, then work with them. Make sure that there is good, consistent and organized research available about any investment you undertake, then work with a partner to create a process for regular review and assessment.

CHAPTER 12

Alternative Approaches to Building
Balanced Stock Portfolios

Other Choices for the More Aggressive Investor

In most of this book we focused on the use of securities research in building individual stock portfolios. Beyond the basic research tools, there are other ways to invest by using index funds, mutual funds and professionally managed accounts. All of these approaches provide different paths to the same end, but we want to point out some issues to consider before you choose the approach or combination of approaches that work best for you.

Individual Professionally-Managed Accounts Versus Mutual Fund Approach

Investors are often confronted with the decisions between investing in a mutual fund and placing their money directly with a professional manager. There is not a single right answer. One is not better than the other in every case. The reason to use either vehicle is to attain professional management and diversification. The decision should be based upon the following points:

1. How large is the portfolio? The amount of money to be committed may be too small to achieve the diversification desired if the investor holds individual stocks with a professional manager. Mutual funds usually provide a broad diversification, however some mutual funds have very concentrated portfolios. Trying to achieve the highest returns, some mutual fund companies and brokerage firms created some very narrowly-focused products. Some of these products have as few as 20 stocks, and the few stocks are highly concentrated in specific parts of the market. These focused products are often referred to as "holders" or "focus" funds.

2. How do you want to manage capital gains? If you own a portfolio of individual stocks, your cost basis is what you paid for the stocks. Should you buy a mutual fund, you may be buying a portfolio that has large embedded capital gains. For example, you might buy a fund at $15 per share with imbedded capital gains of $5 dollars. If the fund appreciates to $20 per share, and the fund manager realizes the capital gains of $5, you will have a tax liability for the capital gain, even if you hold your position. If the fund declines to $10 per share in value, you will have a tax liabil-

ity for the capital gain, even as you realize the loss. Remember that for the taxable investor, after-tax returns are important. Individually-managed portfolios realize capital gains and losses to coordinate with the entire portfolio of investor holdings. There are some mutual funds available for the taxable investor that focus on minimizing tax obligations.

3. Cash flows, both in and out, can affect mutual funds. If enough mutual fund owners redeem shares, the portfolio manager has to sell shares to cover the redemption. The sale may lead to capital gains or losses for which the remaining shareholders are liable, strictly because of the net redemptions.

4. Some objectives are harder to manage with mutual funds. Mutual funds have a stated set of objectives that the manager must use as a guide. The objectives are group objectives. Individual portfolios can be structured better to suit specific individual needs. For example, if an investor is a doctor with large real estate holdings, she might want to avoid further investments in real estate and perhaps some medical industries. It might be difficult to find a fund that matches those specific needs, and meets other goals.

What do I Gain with a Professionally-Managed Account?

Professionally-managed accounts consolidate activities that the investor must undertake. Historically, professionally-managed accounts brought together activities, with two or more institutions participating in providing all of the financial services an investor needed. The first activity of the professional manager is to provide portfolio structure and discretionary investment management. Professional investment managers charge a fee that is based upon a percentage of the assets under management, or they charge a performance fee on excess returns above the stated benchmark, or both. The investor does not participate in the active management of her account, but leaves it to the professional.

Another activity of the asset manager is to execute orders for the portfolio. Normally a separate brokerage firm completes the execution. There have been many cases where the asset manager places orders through his own firms' brokerage arm. The manager is now required by the Securities and Exchange Commission (SEC) to seek out the best priced execution, and a conflict of interest can exist when the manager places orders within his own firm. Nonetheless, order placement is left to the manager's discretion.

Sometimes clients will request that trades be directed to a particular brokerage firm and often to a specific broker. A client and broker may have a relationship that includes comprehensive financial planning, search and selection of investment managers and the monitoring of investment results. By directing trading activity to a particular broker, the broker is paid indirectly so that he can provide services such as Bloomberg reports, performance monitoring and research directly to the investor.

Another activity of the account manager is providing custodian services. Someone has to physically hold the securities, settle transactions, collect dividends and provide a monthly accounting of the activities and balances. Custodian services are normally done by bank custodial services, or are provided by brokerage firms as part of the total services included with order execution.

If a professional manager is retained, the investor will want a regular accounting of how well the manager is performing on an absolute and relative basis, and relative to the benchmark for the stated portfolio objective. Outside consultants provide measures of absolute and relative performance, so that clients can see how their manager is doing relative to others with similar performance objectives. Many of the performance measurement services also provide a ranking of the performance results within a universe of accounts managed for the same objectives. This service provides the investor with information that shows how professional managers perform versus the selected benchmark. The purpose of this performance measure is to provide information to investors so that they are able to maintain a meaningful dialog with both trustees and managers. The information is intended to enhance client/manager discussions. It is not intended to provide information to investors so that they can fire their managers at will.

There is significant evidence that the performance of active mutual fund managers converges over time. In other words, sometimes a manager out-performs, and other times he under-performs. It is a rare manager who always out-performs. Sometimes clients fire managers because of poor performance when in fact it is their management style that is out of favor. It is very unwise to change managers because the "small cap" mandate isn't currently performing. Compare apples to apples and orange to oranges. Changing managers because their portfolio style is unpopular can be very costly over time. If manager performance converges over time, it pays to be contrary. A manager who is currently under-performing has a higher probability of out-performing next year than one who is currently out-performing. As an investor you can choose between investing within index funds, or you can invest with professional managers. Investors should not expect a professionally-managed account always to out-perform the market. However, there are a few managers who rarely perform well and they should be avoided at any cost.

Beyond the convergence issue, there is much discussion about whether or not portfolio managers can add alpha, or excess return, to a portfolio through good individual stock selection. Over certain time periods managers have excelled in stock selection, while over other time periods investors have earned better returns when they purchased index funds. Historically, periods of economic downturns, early recoveries and periods of fundamental structural change all correlate with the success of the individual portfolio manager relative to the index. Between the late 1960s and 1980, managers tended to out-perform their benchmarks. During most of the 1980s and 1990s, managers have struggled to out-perform the market. From about 1999 until the present 2002, individual managers are tending to earn significant excess returns for their clients. The significant events that have transformed the economy of the new millennium will likely play an important role in creating excellent opportunities for skilled managers to out-perform the indices for some time to come.

Alternative Approaches

Do I Have to Choose One Approach?

There are four basic approaches to building portfolios: 1) build a portfolio on your own or with a partner/financial advisor; 2) hire a professional manager to manage the portfolio for you; 3) buy index funds; or 4) buy mutual funds. Rather than choose between the approaches, most investors use a combination of these approaches to build their portfolios, because a combined approach tends to meet their needs more effectively. The main problem with applying different approaches is that it can become difficult to stay focused on a stated investment goal. While the different investments help to diversify the portfolio, the various approaches need to work together to create the overall desired risk/return profile for the investor. Investors often lose sight of the goal when there are too many moving parts.

Many investors deliberately will construct entire investment programs using several investment approaches. This is not a problem unless they miss the forest for the trees. One of the most common problems we see when we look at portfolios that were created with varied approaches is a large imbalance across sector groups while simultaneously displaying high degrees of diversification within specific sector groups. If the portfolio moves too far away from the benchmark, the risk associated with it is significant for most investors. Another similar problem we see is the problem of overlap. Investors may have multiple holdings of the same companies and/or industry and sector holdings. This problem occurs when investors examine the holdings in the parts of their portfolio separately. It can be difficult to comprehensively examine all holdings as part of a single portfolio. Private investments as part of the portfolio tend to make this problem even more severe.

To achieve the best portfolio structure overall, the investor should define her desired objectives and risk tolerance for the entire portfolio. Aggregate the parts of portfolio and evaluate the whole to check for balance and to see if the portfolio is arranged to meet goals and risk postures. The next step should involve creating a core portfolio that meets most of those objectives. The core portfolio can be constructed with individual stocks as discussed in the earlier chapters of this book, or it can be structured with index funds and/or mutual funds that take a core portfolio approach. Another alternative would be to use a professional manager to create a core portfolio for you. After creating the core portfolio that addresses your basic goals, the investor can round out the portfolio with global or international mutual funds, sector funds, large, mid or small cap funds and/or country funds to achieve the correct balance.

A tool like Morningstar's Instant X-ray can help the investor avoid the perils associated with complicated portfolios. The Instant X-ray tool can handle individual investments as well as the entire aggregated portfolio. This tool is very helpful in discerning whether certain investments are contributing to diversification or moving to portfolio away from the benchmark. The tool identifies investment over-laps, and provides portfolio sector weights that the investor can check against goals.

Conclusion

The investment approaches discussed in the chapter provide many ways to achieve similar results. Each investor should have a plan, and then build his overall portfolio by using the approaches, keeping in mind the goal of achieving an aggregated portfolio that meets his goals. The aggregated portfolio should meet risk tolerance and portfolio style objectives. Monitor the aggregated portfolio over the short-term, but with a long-term focus to ensure that as it changes over time and is adjusted to maintain the desired overall structure.

CONCLUSION

A geography professor ends the semester by writing a final exam question on the white board. The exam question reads, "How do you get to Chicago?" Most of the students spend the next hour writing furiously in their blue books, providing detailed information about routes to Chicago. One student writes a quick answer in his blue book, turns it in to the professor, and leaves the classroom. After class, a small group of students talk about the guy who left early. "He must not have known much about geography," they say. When the students receive their blue books from the professor, they are amazed at the failing grades they receive. One student, the guy who left early, is smiling. His correct answer, "It depends from where you are starting!" has received a passing grade.

This story points to an important concept for investors. Understand where you are and where you want to go with your investments. Establish your goals and objectives for your investments, consider your time horizon, return requirements and degree of risk aversion. We recommend that investors maintain a fully invested, sector neutral portfolio, but investors may choose to create decision rules that determine the percentage of the overall portfolio invested in equities. We use the S & P 500 as a benchmark, but investors can use the same approach to maintaining a balanced portfolio with virtually any benchmark

Learn about securities research. The starting place for excellent long-run returns involves knowing the nature of your portfolio, its structure, its risk characteristics and the active bets being placed. What investments are contributing to the portfolios excess returns?

Once you know where you are and you know where you want to go, you have to make some decisions. Will you work alone? If so, how will you establish a consistent set of investment disciplines? Do you have access to high quality research from strategists and analysts? Do you have a source to provide price data and descriptive statistics about market sectors, industries and companies?

We have made the case in this book that it is difficult to go it alone. Some investors work well on their own, but many who try investing on their own have very bad results. Individual investors often take on far too much risk, turn over their portfolios too often, tend to concentrate on individual stocks and get excited about last year's favorites. If you don't want to go it alone, what kind of a partnership arrangement do you want to estab-

Conclusion

lish? Whether you choose to work with a professional manager, invest in mutual funds or work with a financial advisor, it makes sense to manage your wealth using the advice of qualified professionals.

We want to conclude this book with three key points to successful investing. The first point is to become educated. Never stop learning, because the market will continue to innovate. We think that this book is a good resource for educating oneself. A smart investor looks for information about changing trends and comprehensive investment practices. Whether investors use mutual funds or hire professional managers, they need tools to select and monitor the people managing their investments. This book provides a set of tools for doing so and an organized manner for continuing the process of education.

Remember that much of the research available to investors focuses on individual stocks, but there are sources of sector and industry research available through large brokerage firms and specialty research shops. Create a process to use research that has produced good results. Use the information of the strategist along with the research of the analyst. Check the recommendations with a source that provides information on market sentiment, such as relative strength analysis. Don't invest money based upon hot stock tips, web sites or magazines' recommended lists.

Beyond identifying the sources of research, learn to use those sources effectively. The process involves identifying important and useful information in order to achieve your desired results. We have shown you distinct categories of research and how to use them in a step-by-step process toward investment success. Use research effectively and for its desired purpose. A hammer can break apart a board, and a saw will pound in a nail, but the effort expended is too great. Once you have created your investment "tool box," use it effectively.

The next key to successful investing is to diversify risks. There are traditional ways to diversify and there are more complex ways to do so. If you have a traditional long stock portfolio, diversification occurs as you "hug" the benchmark. Your holdings are spread across market sectors and industries and in this manner you diversify specific risks. In order to earn excess returns, or alpha, you over-weight and under-weight specific sectors and industries and you focus your individual stock research on the best companies in those sectors and industries expected to out-perform the market. In this manner you expose yourself to specific risks with the expectation that those risks will reap higher than market returns.

Finally, we think that most investors need a partner for investing success. A professional will provide information, insight, and counsel. Any partnership produces according to the skills of the individual members. Nothing replaces experience and demonstrable skill. The process of managing the information around your portfolio can be detailed and time consuming. Remember the concept of comparative advantage. If you are a physician, your time is better spent in your medical practice than weeding through tables of analyst reports. If your skills are in the area of finance and investing, you may want to manage the information yourself, but even then you need access to certain types of information that brokers have available. A financial advisor focuses his career and time on finance. A good advisor will be educated and experienced. He will have time and energy and interest to devote to your portfolio. Research shows that investors who work with professionals earn better returns than those who go it alone.

We believe that investing should be a team effort. Two important things to investors are their health and their wealth. Most people use health information on Web sites and in magazines to educate themselves and to facilitate dialog with their doctors. In the same way, we believe that Web sites and public sources of financial information are useful for investors to self-educate, but should not be used as primary sources of information or as rationale to go it alone. Working with a partner can produce better results. Use the information provided in this book, find a long-term partner, educate yourself and diversify to get the risk-adjusted results you want by creating a winning portfolio.

ENDNOTES

General Note: *The examples in this book were constructed based upon many sources. In most examples where we borrowed from outside sources, we edited the text to make our points clear. We would like to acknowledge Goldman Sachs Research, Merrill Lynch Research, Value Line and Morningstar as sources for our exhibits, but note that few of the exhibits provide identical information from these sources.*

Chapter 1. The Democratization of Wall Street

[1] Mary Farrell, <u>Beyond the Basics</u>, Simon & Shuster, 2000

Chapter 2. Diversification, Asset Allocation and Risk

[1] Based upon a normal distribution. We understand that there is much evidence against the assumption that stocks are distributed normally, but this is a simple illustration. We are not undertaking hypothesis testing.

[2] The S & P 500 includes large cap value and growth stocks, and represents 85 percent of the American market and 50 percent of the world market, thus it is our measure of the market.

[3] Source: Goldman Sachs Asset Management, 2001

[4] Jeremy Siegel, Stocks for the Long Run, 2nd edition, McGraw Hill, 1998

Chapter 4. Portfolio Styles

[1] Some argue that the Peter Lynch Ratio – the sum of the growth rate of the stock's earnings plus dividend yield/ P/E ratio indicates that these stocks were a good deal.

Chapter 5. How Do We Begin?

[1] The information used to construct Exhibits 5-3 and 5-4 was gathered from Standard & Poors's Web site (www.standardandpoors.com) during 2001. This type of information is generally available to the public.

[2] The G.E. example is not an isolated one. Examples of other single company industries have been: 1) Long Term Health Care: Manor Care, Inc. at 0.013% of index, and 2) Defense Electronics: Raytheon Co. at 0.052% of index.

Chapter 6. The Use of Technical Analysis

[1] Biaks, Klaas, et. al., "Mutual Fund Performance: An

Empirical Decomposition into Stock-Picking Talent, Style, Transactions Costs, and Expenses." <u>Journal of Finance</u>, Vol 55, Issue 4: 1655-1705.

[2] All charts discussed in this chapter are available at The Quantum Group's Web site, *www.quantum relativestrength.com*

Chapter 10. Following Your Portfolio Over Time

[1] <u>A Woman's Guide to Investing</u>, Virginia B. Morris and Kenneth M. Morris, Lightbulb Press, 1988.

Chapter 11. Global and Zero Correlation Investments

[1] Recent changes in the global index to GDP weighting have worked to address this problem.

INDEX OF CHARTS
AND EXHIBITS

Chapter	*Exhibit/Chart*	*Page*

Index of Charts and Exhibits

INDEX

Symbols

A

Index

Index

Index

Index

Index